KU-540-695

FEDEGRAPHICA

MARK HODGKINSON is a tennis author and journalist. His other books include *You Cannot be Serious!, Game, Set and Match: Secret Weapons of the World's Top Tennis Players, Andy Murray: Wimbledon Champion* and *Ivan Lendl: The Man Who Made Murray*. He has written for GQ, the ATP, the WTA, Wimbledon.com, ESPN and the Daily Telegraph.

Brimming with creative inspiration, how-to projects and useful information to enrich your everyday life, Quarto Knows is a favourite destination for those pursuing their interests and passions. Visit our site and dig deeper with our books into your area of interest: Quarto Creates, Quarto Cooks, Quarto Homes, Quarto Lives, Quarto Drives, Quarto Explores, Quarto Gifts, or Quarto Kids.

PICTURE CREDITS

Shutterstock (Neale Cousland) 3, 56, 120-121, (Evren Kalinbacak) 60, (lev radin) 87, 215, (Leonard Zhukovsky) 99, (meunierd) 109; Getty Images (Amin Mohammad Jamali) 5, (Clive Brunskill) 15, 20-21, 39, 40-41, 58-59, 69, 82, 83, 84-85, 100-101, 103, 106-107, 134, 176-177, 203, 204-205, 252-253, (Clive Brunskill/Getty Images for Nike) 223, (Julian Finney) 12-13, 72-73, 156, 164-165, 230-231, 232, (Ron C. Angle) 31, (Jean-Loup Gautreau/AFP) 35, (GREG WOOD/AFP) 151, (BERTRAND GUAY/AFP) 158, (WILLIAM WEST/AFP) 184, (CARL DE SOUZA/AFP) 211, (CARMEN JASPERSEN/AFP) 217, (JAVIER SORIANO/AFP) 244, (Bob Thomas) 43, (Justin Setterfield) 48, (Sean Garnsworthy) 63, (ODD ANDERSEN/AFP) 65, (Al Bello) 66-67, 180, 203, (Mike Hewitt) 70-71 (Popperfoto) 77, (Tommy Hindley/Professional Sport/Popperfoto) 128-129, (PATRICK KOVARIK/AFP) 92, (Ryan Pierse) 96-97, (Bongarts) 114, 238, (Alex Livesey) 124-125, (Bob Martin/Sports Illustrated) 127, 166, (Manny Millan/Sports Illustrated) 138-139, 147, (Simon Bruty /Sports Illustrated) 148-149, (ATP) 141, (Cynthia Lum) 144, (Laurent ZABULON/Gamma-Rapho) 159, (Maddie Meyer) 190-191, 198, (Jan Kruger) 192, (Ian Walton) 195, (Wayne Taylor) 208-209, (Peter Staples/ATP World Tour) 212, (Peter Kramer) 222, (David Cannon for Dubai Duty Free) 226-227, (ChinaFotoPress/ChinaFotoPres) 234-235, (The Roger Federer Foundation) 237, (David M. Benett/Getty Images for Moët & Chandon) 242, (Clive Brunskill/Staff) 271; Alamy (Action Plus Sports Image/Alamy Stock Photo) 7, 11, 179, 255, 258; Corbis (Ben Radford) 89, 153, 168-169, (Neil Tingle/Loop Images) 154-155, (Michele Eve/Splash News) 189; Roger Federer 27; Mirrorpix 172.

DATA SOURCES

Where applicable, data is correct up to the end of the 2017 season. Official Wimbledon data from I.B.M. (2015 tournament) 18-19, 32, 75, 192, (2002-2017) 182; Official I.B.M. data from the four Grand Slams 24, 33, 90-91, 96-97, 116-117, 186; Official I.B.M. data (2003-2017) 37; Official data from the ATP World Tour 25, 29, 39, 54, 59, 76, 79, 80-81, 110-111, 113, 120-121, 124-125, 157, 160-161, 163, 175, 196-197, 201, 214, 218-219, 260, 264-265, (and other sources) 171, (and DavisCup.com) 230-231; Data from videographer John Yandell 46-47, 72; Data from tennis analyst Damien Saunder 50-51, 104-105; Official data from the International Tennis Federation 118, 142, 160-161, 167; Data from Forbes Magazine 240-241, 244; Data from The Roger Federer Foundation 250.

This updated edition first published in 2018 by
Aurum Press
an imprint of The Quarto Group
The Old Brewery
6 Blundell Street
London N7 9BH
United Kingdom
www.QuartoKnows.com

© Quarto Publishing plc. 2016, 2018
Text © Mark Hodgkinson 2016, 2018

Mark Hodgkinson has asserted his moral right to be identified as the Author of this Work in accordance with the Copyright Designs and Patents Act 1988.

All rights reserved. No part of this book may be reproduced or utilised in any form or by any means, electronic or mechanical, including photocopying, recording or by any information storage and retrieval system, without permission in writing from Aurum Press.

Every effort has been made to trace the copyright holders of material quoted in this book. If application is made in writing to the publisher, any omissions will be included in future editions.

A catalogue record for this book is available from the British Library.

ISBN 978 1 78131 758 7

10 9 8 7 6 5 4 3 2 1
2020 2019 2018

Design: www.fogdog.co.uk
Infographics by Paul Oakley and Nick Clark
Printed in China

FEDEGRAPHICA

A GRAPHIC BIOGRAPHY OF THE GENIUS OF ROGER FEDERER

MARK HODGKINSON

CONTENTS

'YOU'RE WATCHING TRUE GENIUS.
HE'S THE GREATEST PLAYER
THAT'S EVER LIVED.'

JOHN McENROE

PROLOGUE

Backstage at The O2 Arena in south-east London for the finale to the 2017 season, the interior design of Roger Federer's personal dressing-room was an elegant reminder of his astonishing resurgence. Covering one of the walls of his room were photographs of some of his finest moments of the year. Along the corridor, where the other seven players at the eight-man ATP Finals also had the rare luxury of their own private space rather than sharing a locker-room, there were more individual memory walls. But with Federer the designer could have gone much further, and papered the entire room with feel-good images.

Perhaps more than any other sport, tennis specialises in comebacks. That is no bad thing: comebacks often make the best stories, with soaring, uplifting narrative arcs that can moisten the eyes of even the most emotionally buttoned-up. It is a crowded field: Andre Agassi pulling himself out of a spiral down the rankings, or Kim Clijsters returning from maternity leave to win multiple Grand Slams, to name just two. But Federer's comeback in 2017 was perhaps the most astounding of them all. However, it was also so much more than a comeback. Federer went beyond chasing old highs and rediscovering old form on the tennis court; incredibly, in the year he turned thirty-six, he was touching new heights.

The assembly of the world's best players in Greenwich in November 2017 provided the ideal occasion to reflect on what had been a tennis year of the gloriously unexpected. Federer's rejuvenation was repeatedly described as a tennis time warp: it was as if Peak Roger, who was supposedly around from 2004-07 when he was in his mid-twenties, had been transported to the modern day. But the reality was even more exhilarating than that: ten years on, he was playing the best tennis of his life. No wonder, while sitting in his dressing-room before matches, he was often laughing, joking and drinking coffee. While other competitors fussed and fretted before walking out through the clouds of dry-ice and on to court, Federer was simply at peace.

One of the images on the wall was from the Australian Open. When Federer arrived at Melbourne Park in January 2017, he was returning from what had been the longest break of his career, some six months, while he recovered from a knee

injury. By winning his first major in five years, the Roger Federer of 2017 revealed himself to be, in many ways, a superior player to Peak Roger. With Federer defeating Rafa Nadal for the title, and Serena and Venus Williams contesting the women's final, the Australian Open became known as the Flashback Slam. But it would be wrong to think of this as pure tennis retro. Later in the year Federer would add an unprecedented eighth Wimbledon title to extend his record to nineteen Grand Slams. To fully appreciate the wonder, spirit, boldness and brilliance of Federer's play in 2017, you had to understand that you were watching him in his absolute prime.

Federer's peers looked on with admiration and voted him Comeback Player of the Year in the ATP World Tour Awards. In addition to the two majors, he landed trophies in Indian Wells, Miami, Halle, Shanghai and Basel. That made seven titles in all, more than anyone else, and the most tournaments he had won in a season since 2007. With fifty-two match victories, and just five defeats, his winning percentage of 91.2 was also higher than anyone else on tour. Never before had Federer won as much as $13.1 million in one year, and this in a season when, by his own admission, he was 'only playing part-time'.

He even threatened to return to number one in the world rankings, and would have been the oldest man in history to do so had he succeeded. Only Nadal, also rebooted after a mediocre 2016, finished above him. And that after Federer chose to skip the entire clay-court season. From early April to the middle of June, he did not play at all. He appeared at three of the four Grand Slams, and just four of the nine Masters tournaments, yet still ended the year on 9,605 ranking points, little more than one thousand points short of Nadal on 10,645. By contrast, Nadal played all four majors and all nine Masters. To put Federer's year further into context, Grigor Dimitrov, the twenty-six-year-old Bulgarian who used to be known as 'Baby Fed' because of his similar style of play, finished the season at number three with around half the Swiss' total.

'Roger is a better player today than ever before,' said Federer's former coach, Paul Annacone, while Pete Sampras, a winner of fourteen majors, was taken aback by his friend's level and results: 'Roger had a magical season in 2017 – he's one of those freaks of nature who comes around every fifty years, and he can do things that no one else can do. What he did, the year he turned thirty-six, was incredible – he actually improved.' Federer knew he had to refresh his game, and was willing to do so. 'Roger doesn't view change and adjustment as a shock to his system – he knows he has the talent to adapt and he's very happy to make those changes,' said Annacone.

Bizarrely, this regeneration started with a foaming, bubbling bath in a

Melbourne hotel suite. Federer's 2017 season would have played out quite differently had it not been for an accident following his semi-final defeat at the previous year's Australian Open. Running a bath for his children, Federer turned and felt a 'click' in his knee. It resulted in the first operation of his career. He returned to competition, but did not win a title all season, the first time that had happened since 2000. Indeed, the Wimbledon Championships produced a moment, and an image, that looked like it might come to define Federer's later years: after losing his footing during the semi-final defeat by Milos Raonic, he ended up lying face down on the Centre Court grass. That would be his last appearance of the season. He used the remainder of the year to rest and strengthen his body. Practice weeks in Dubai and Switzerland provided the opportunity to work on his game: to innovate in a way that only he can, blending the classic with the highly progressive and ultra-modern.

Changing rackets in 2014 had been a ballsy move, which at the time almost felt like he was starting out again. But more progressive was 2015's creation of a new shot, a half-volley service return hit just short of the service line, that he called 'Sneak Attack by Roger', 'S.A.B.R.' for short, or 'Fed Attack'. For years, Federer's tennis had been the closest that the sport had come to performance art with his cinematic flicks of the racket, those through-the-legs tweeners and other trickery. But this was the first time he had been such a risk-taker. When Federer played the shot, and then dashed into the net looking for a volley, there was a danger of him looking like a fool. But it could also work beautifully. Borderline confrontational, the S.A.B.R. could leave opponents discombobulated. This one shot changed how he saw his tennis.

That desire to take a more attacking approach continued, and intensified, on the practice court as he prepared for 2017. The result was a futuristic, aggressive remodelling of his single-handed backhand. Once, Federer would have been minded to slice most of his backhand returns, which often allowed his opponent to take control of the point. But, by coming over the ball when striking his backhand return, he could be the one to take the initiative.

It may sound a simple change but in fact it was a significant technical switch, and more importantly revealed a shift in psyche: the inhibitions had disappeared, he was playing with freedom, maybe even abandon. In this shot it was possible to detect the influence of S.A.B.R. Some observers felt that those upgrades to his backhand also led to improvements in his whole game. With greater confidence in his backhand, there was a more balanced feel to his tennis. Federer's movement had always been exceptional, but now with less reliance on his forehand, it seemed even better. As Patrick Mouratoglou, Serena Williams's coach, and an astute analyst of the game, observed: '[Federer] worked on his backhand so he can take the ball earlier than before, which is a big change – the ball he hits is faster. The type of tennis he was playing before he made those changes, he wouldn't have won another slam. It was courageous to adapt. But that's why champions are champions, as they are always trying to improve.'

It all came together at Wimbledon. All around Federer at the 2017 Championships others were struggling, whether mentally or physically. Andy Murray (hip), Novak Djokovic (elbow) and Marin Čilić (blister) were not at their best, while the younger Bernard Tomic said he had been 'bored' on court. Nadal, Federer's perennial rival, meanwhile, did not go deep into the draw. Over the fortnight, Federer's abilities, and enduring love for the sport, seemed to intensify as he beat Čilić in the final to surpass the record of seven Wimbledon titles he had shared with Sampras and William Renshaw, a champion from the Victorian era. 'Physically and mentally, Roger still wants to be out there, and that's incredible at his age,' said Sampras. 'He has been playing just the right amount to stay fresh. He still enjoys the travel and loves the game.'

Federer did not win the season's finale at The O2 Arena. He was the oldest competitor in the history of the tournament, though, and his longevity such that the man who beat him in the semi-finals, Belgium's David Goffin, used to have a poster of Federer on his bedroom wall.

The author J.M. Coetzee once described Federer as 'something like the human ideal made visible'. Coetzee also found that 'one starts by envying Federer, one moves from there to admiring him, and one ends up neither envying nor admiring him but exalted at the revelation of what a human being – a being like oneself – can do'. Another novelist, David Foster Wallace, thought of Federer as 'a creature whose body is both flesh and, somehow, light', and wrote of what he called 'Federer Moments': 'These are the times, as you watch the young Swiss play, when the jaw drops and eyes protrude and sounds are made that bring spouses in from other rooms to see if you are OK.'

Coetzee and Foster Wallace were both writing in what used to be thought of as Federer's golden years, a decade earlier. They could not have imagined that Federer's true peak would come so many seasons later, the year he turned thirty-six.

At its core, Federer's story is about the pursuit of greatness. With every uninhibited swing of his racket in 2017, and then when winning his twentieth Grand Slam title at the 2018 Australian Open, he kept strengthening his status as the greatest of all time.

Where applicable, data is correct up until the end of the 2017 season, unless otherwise stated.

1
CRAZY
MANIAC

CALL IT ROGER FEDERER'S PAVLOV'S DOG EXPERIMENT;
THIS IS A SECRET STUDY, INVOLVING A RACKET, A BALL
AND A SALIVATING OPPONENT WAITING TO RECEIVE SERVE.
YET IT'S ALL HIDDEN IN PLAIN SIGHT ON CENTRE COURT.

So much of serving, and therefore of tennis, is about disguise, deception and surprise. Andre Agassi tells the story – and don't let anyone suggest this is apocryphal – of how he would read Boris Becker's serve just by looking at his tongue. As Becker tossed the ball up, he would unwittingly stick his tongue out – 'a tiny red arrow', Agassi called it – pointing in the direction in which he was about to take fire. Even before the ball had left Becker's strings, Agassi could start following that arrow. To think that Becker, unknowingly sabotaged by his subconscious mind, would inspire Federer, who has learned to condition and manipulate the receiver. Supposedly secret – his rivals seem to be unaware that this is happening, and how they are being 'played' – Federer's ongoing experiment is available for all to see, if only you know what to look for. Here, serve by Pavlovian serve, is confirmation of how the Swiss underwent the greatest transformation that the sport has ever seen. From young and troubled artist, perfectionist and hothead raging by the Rhine – and making a noise halfway between a yodel and a primal scream – to thinker, strategist and arch-manipulator. Think of Federer's ball-toss as the tennis equivalent of Pavlov's bell, triggering the responses he has conditioned in his opponent. Maybe we should call it Federer's Pavlov's Dog Experiment, this secret study, involving a racket, a ball and a salivating opponent waiting to receive serve. Yet it is all hidden in plain sight on Centre Court.

It is tempting to romanticise Federer's beautiful tennis, and to believe he plays primarily, if not purely, on instinct. The truth is, he appears to think more about the strategies of tennis than anyone else in the sport. 'It might surprise people to know that Roger is very pattern-orientated, with those patterns

▶ Federer uses the same ball toss and body position on every serve.

changing based on the score,' said Craig O'Shannessy, the lead analyst for the ATP World Tour, who has also advised Novak Djokovic on strategy.

The aim for Federer is not to be considered unpredictable, and for his opponent to be entirely reliant on guesswork. No, far better to create an illusion in his opponent's head that they know which serve is coming. Federer wants his opponents to believe – wrongly, of course – that they can predict the future. 'He sticks to his patterns, and they are strong, recognisable patterns,' said O'Shannessy, who has studied Federer's serve for years. 'This goes back to the theory of Pavlov's Dog. Some people seem to think that in tennis you want a shotgun or scattergun approach, that it should be very random. But you don't want that because you can't control that. You'll start to second-guess yourself. You won't be quite sure what you're supposed to be doing next, and you'll go for a low percentage shot on a really important point and it just catches up with you. What you want is Pavlov's Dog. You want to ring the bell and for the opponent to expect a certain response. You're conditioning their responses and their minds and then you can manipulate them.'

'SOME PEOPLE SEEM TO THINK THAT IN TENNIS YOU WANT A SHOTGUN OR SCATTERGUN APPROACH, THAT IT SHOULD BE VERY RANDOM. BUT YOU DON'T WANT THAT BECAUSE YOU CAN'T CONTROL THAT.'

Most players, O'Shannessy disclosed, are hurt by their self-obsession. Not Federer. 'Roger is always inside his opponent's mind. With Roger, a hidden element of his brilliance is the constant awareness of what his opponent is expecting and thinking. Most players think they should be focusing on their strokes, and they believe, "It's all about me". It's not. That's only true when you are at the beginner level of tennis, not among the elite. The most important thing on a tennis court is the person on the other side of the net. You don't necessarily need to play well – you just need to have your opponent playing badly. Get inside their mind and figure out what they're thinking.'

There are times, though, such as in the semi-final of the 2015 Wimbledon Championships, when it is perfectly clear to everybody, and not just to Federer, what his opponent is thinking. That afternoon on Centre Court, Andy Murray called out in the direction of his coach, Amélie Mauresmo: 'What do you want me to do?' The rules about illegal mid-match coaching prevented Mauresmo from responding, but what could she have said? In truth, there was nothing that an exasperated Murray could have done differently in the face of Federer's greatest serving performance for years. Bjorn Borg would say it was the best he had seen Federer serve for 'maybe ten years', while Murray would suggest: 'It was Roger's best serving performance in one of our matches, and not just by a little bit, but by far.' All this just a month before Federer turned thirty-four. As Federer was applauded all the way back to the locker room for the first time he could remember, there was confirmation of the truth that everything flows from his serve. For all the majesty in other parts of Federer's game, he would not have won all those Grand Slam titles if it was not for this shot, the one capable of reducing his opponents to Pavlovian dogs. That summer Federer won 116 successive service games, a run that started in Halle and ended at the All England Club. So impregnable had Federer's serve become that when he was finally broken, in his Wimbledon quarter-final against Frenchman Gilles Simon, the Reuters agency put out a 'Breaking News' alert.

For Federer to condition his opponents into thinking they know where he is about to serve, when of course they do not, it is important he has no 'tell' on his toss or any other part of his service motion which might disclose the truth. Most players have one, even if it is not as marked as Becker's. It is perfectly possible, when receiving most elite players' serves, to study the position of the ball-toss and to predict – often with something approaching certainty – where they are about to serve. To offer one example, if a right-handed player is serving from the deuce side, and he tosses the ball further to his right, you can be fairly sure the ball will fizz wide. That knowledge gives you, the receiver, an additional few hundredths of a second to react to the serve, and that can be the difference between an ace and a return winner smoked down the line. But these are not clues that Federer offers up; there is no giveaway with him.

'Roger can hit every serve with the same ball-toss, and with such high precision, and that's what makes it so difficult against him. You don't know where the ball is going to go, and then suddenly he hits the line,' said Toni Nadal, Rafa's uncle and coach. 'So Roger tosses the ball up and you are looking for signs, always looking for signs, but the ball-toss is the same, and the body position is the same, wherever he is hitting the ball. Then, right at the last moment, Roger changes and sends the ball wide, or down the "T" or wherever he wants to hit it. You don't have any of the signs that you get with other players.'

As Pete Sampras, one of Federer's boyhood idols and now one of his

SERVICE DIRECTION: THE IMPORTANCE OF FEDERER'S SERVING PATTERNS

Case study based on official data from the 2015 Wimbledon Championships

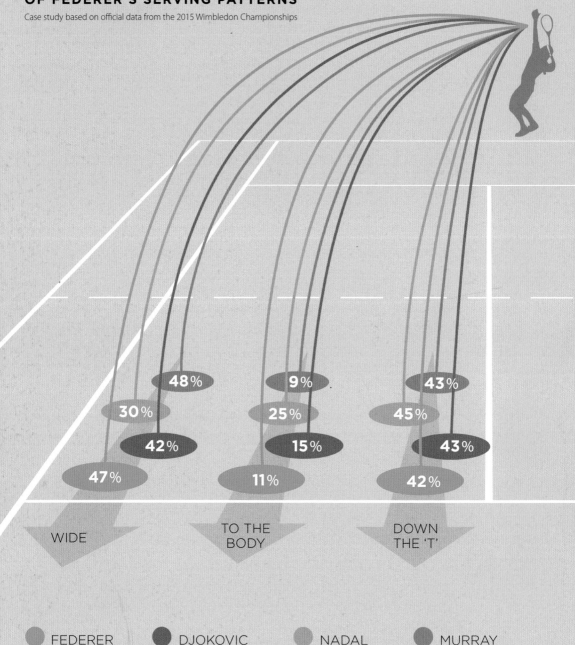

WIDE

48%
30%
42%
47%

TO THE BODY

9%
25%
15%
11%

DOWN THE 'T'

43%
45%
43%
42%

FEDERER   DJOKOVIC   NADAL   MURRAY

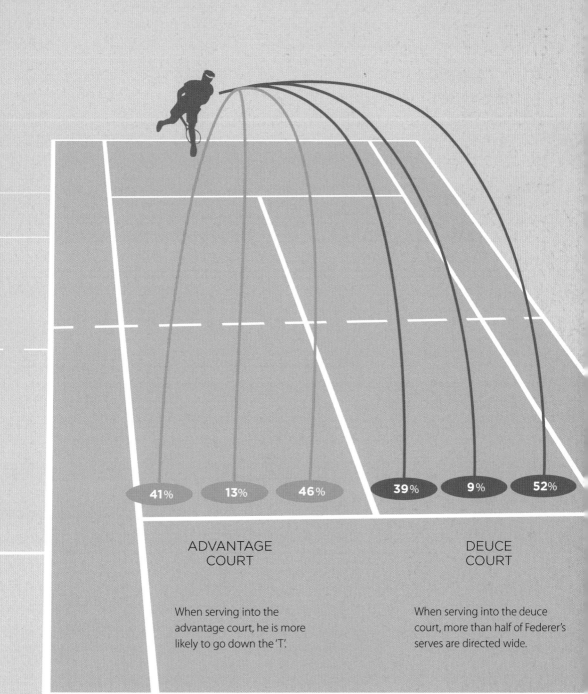

41% **13%** **46%** **39%** **9%** **52%**

ADVANTAGE
COURT

DEUCE
COURT

When serving into the
advantage court, he is more
likely to go down the 'T'.

When serving into the deuce
court, more than half of Federer's
serves are directed wide.

www.wimbledon.org

119
mph

◀ Federer likes to play quickly - he has been known to win service games inside a minute.

firmest friends in tennis, said: 'Roger doesn't have a huge serve, but he has a very good first serve that sets up the point.' Federer's serve should not be viewed in isolation; instead think of the serve and Federer's next shot as a package. 'What makes Roger so great is that he can make his opponent return the ball to a part of the court which then allows Roger to dictate. He combines the strength of his first serve with the strength of the first shot that follows,' O'Shannessy said.

For the first point of the game, Federer tends to go wide. 'That means he's serving to the right-hander's forehand, but you will never put a forehand under more pressure than when you hit a wide serve and have them stretching for it. It diminishes what is typically a strength and makes it almost a weakness,' O'Shannessy said. 'The opponent is going to try to hit the ball back to Roger's backhand. But they're on the defensive so they're not going to feel as though they can go down the line, as that's too risky. So they tend to play the ball back towards Roger's backhand side, but much closer to the centre of the court. They are giving themselves more margin, but that means Roger probably won't have to move more than two metres to reach that ball. So he's going to run around that backhand and play an aggressive forehand. That's a tactic he uses a lot. He's just the master at that.'

SO IMPREGNABLE HAD FEDERER'S SERVE BECOME THAT WHEN HE WAS FINALLY BROKEN, IN HIS WIMBLEDON QUARTER-FINAL AGAINST FRENCHMAN GILLES SIMON, THE REUTERS AGENCY PUT OUT A 'BREAKING NEWS' ALERT.

When Federer is 'hitting his spots', Tim Henman said, it becomes fiendishly difficult to 'get the ball away from the middle of the court'. The forehand that follows completes 'Roger's classic one-two punch'. For a right-hander, such as Federer, serving wide into the advantage court is the hardest ball to land, which is why most players tend to prefer walloping it down the 'T'. Yet, at 15–love, Federer will direct a lot of balls wide, to the right-hander's backhand. During the 2015 Wimbledon Championships, forty-one per cent of his serves into that court went wide, which is a considerably higher percentage than most. Federer considers this to be a high-percentage strategy as it allows him to open up a hole on the forehand side.

It gets interesting at 30–love. 'At that stage in the game, Roger's opponent is conditioned to think that the ball is going wide, so Roger goes down the "T",' O'Shannessy said. 'Roger will always be thinking about the score and also, "Where does my opponent think the ball is going to go?" If Roger has

BUT HOW MANY OTHER PLAYERS ARE CAPABLE OF HITTING SO MANY 'SOFT' ACES, WHEN THE BALL HARDLY MAKES A SOUND AS IT MAKES CONTACT WITH THE WALL?

been doing his Pavlov's Dog serves, by going wide on the first couple of points, the "T" is going to be wide open. Now, is he going to be aiming at a beach towel or a face cloth? If Roger's opponent thinks that the ball is going down the "T", and the score's 15–40, then it's a face cloth. But if it's 30–love, and he had been wide and wide on the first two points of the game, it's a beach towel. He can probably hit anywhere on that beach towel and it's probably going to be an ace or a return error. Or, at the very least, a weak ball.'

It is when Federer is in command of the service game that he introduces his secondary patterns. 'At 40–love, Roger is almost never going to hit his favourite serve,' said O'Shannessy. 'He's going to use a secondary tactic as he's throwing in the illusion of a mix. If he loses that point, it doesn't matter so much. The points in tennis are not weighted the same. He's probably hitting a bigger serve or he's hitting a jam into the body, something he doesn't do that often. That's when the curve-balls come, when he's ahead and can afford to lose points.'

Remarkably, opponents do not pick up on Federer's ploys, perhaps because he plays at such speed, on occasion winning service games inside a minute. It was revealing to hear Henman still stick to the line that Federer has 'no patterns' on his serve. Years later, Henman is still unaware he was conditioned and manipulated. 'It's interesting you can be running what seem like obvious patterns and opponents just don't realise what is happening,' O'Shannessy said. 'And once Roger gets ahead in that guessing game, he just can't be broken. If the opponent gets on it, Roger can always change it up, but I've never seen that happen. Most players don't understand. Roger is just very good at the subtleties and nuances of this game.'

Of course, deception is nothing without accuracy. Where is the benefit in running these patterns if you cannot hit your spots? Federer can place the ball pretty much wherever he pleases. His smooth service action has allowed him to be extraordinarily consistent and to keep his first-serve percentage so high. 'At difficult moments, on the big points, Roger always gets the ball in,' Toni Nadal said. In the summer of 2010, during the days before the US Open, video footage was leaked on to the internet that supposedly caught him goofing around between takes on the set of a sponsor's shoot, knocking a bottle off a male assistant's head with a William Tell-style serve. That it took so many so

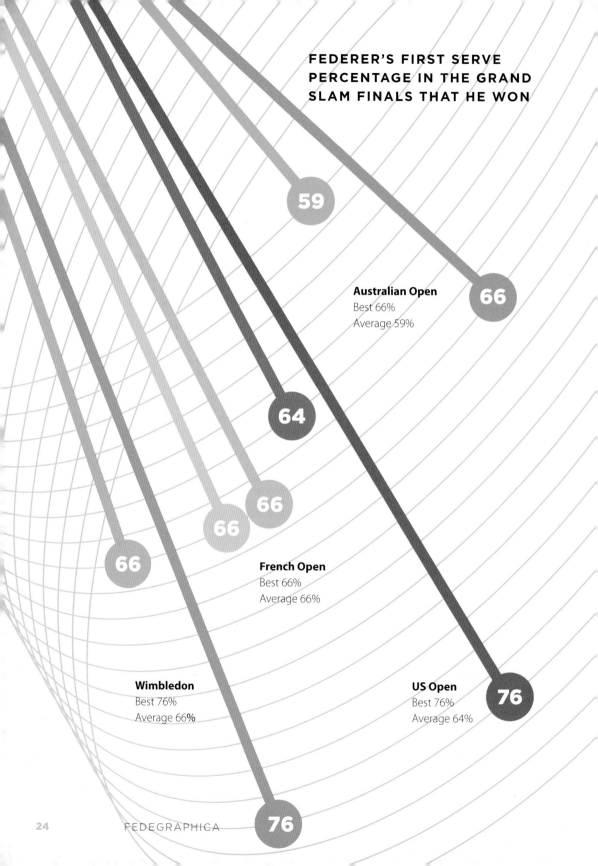

FEDERER'S FIRST SERVE PERCENTAGE IN THE GRAND SLAM FINALS THAT HE WON

59

66

Australian Open
Best 66%
Average 59%

64

66

66

66

French Open
Best 66%
Average 66%

76

Wimbledon
Best 76%
Average 66%

US Open
Best 76%
Average 64%

76

CAREER FIRST SERVE PERCENTAGE

MODERN PLAYERS

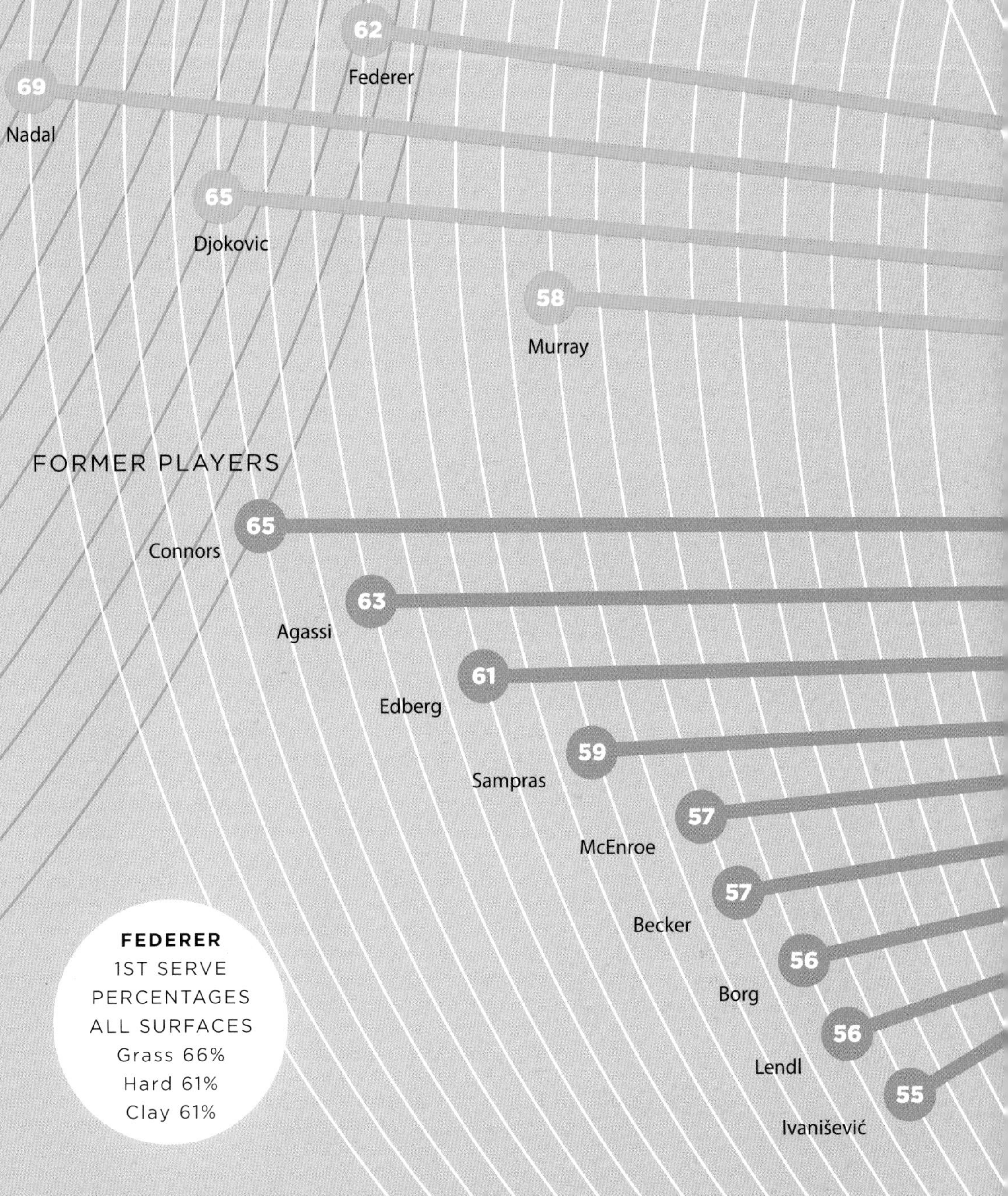

62 Federer

69 Nadal

65 Djokovic

58 Murray

FORMER PLAYERS

65 Connors

63 Agassi

61 Edberg

59 Sampras

57 McEnroe

57 Becker

56 Borg

56 Lendl

55 Ivanišević

FEDERER
1ST SERVE
PERCENTAGES
ALL SURFACES
Grass 66%
Hard 61%
Clay 61%

long to realise that some clever editing had been involved said much about Federer's reputation for precision.

Tennis has an obsession with big serves. It is an understandable obsession: there is something almost primal about a ball travelling at speeds in excess of 150 m.p.h., sometimes reaching 160 m.p.h. For some players, like Australian Sam Groth, who once fired a 163 m.p.h. serve, speed really is everything. But that is patently not true of Federer's serve. Not that Federer's serve is on the slow side. Data from the 2015 Wimbledon Championships demonstrated that the veteran Federer was serving bigger than his rivals in their twenties, with his first serve averaging 118 m.p.h. Federer also does not roll in his second serve, which means that the spins have even more bite, whether that is a slice serve out wide or a kicker rearing up at an opponent's throat.

The thwack of a 130 m.p.h. ace hitting the backstop is as satisfying for Federer as for anyone else. But how many other players are capable of hitting so many 'soft' aces, when the ball hardly makes a sound as it makes contact with the wall? His most impressive aces are when he takes the pace off; his 'slow-motion aces' were once judged by the *Guardian* to be Federer's 'brightest jewels'. During the 2009 Wimbledon final Federer served fifty aces – a record for a title-match there – and while many of those were struck with maximum power, a sizeable number were not. He does not need to club the ball past an opponent; he can have them swinging at fresh air by manipulating their mind. 'By taking some pace off, Roger can make sure he lands the serve and he has the benefit, thanks to his Pavlov's Dog serves, of the opponent not being there waiting,' O'Shannessy said. 'He makes an opponent lean one way, and as a returner if you lean one way, you're completely giving up the other way. It's almost impossible then to cover the other side. Roger looks great serving those slow aces. But let's say that ace comes at 30–all – he would have set up that ace earlier in the game with his serve locations so that when the bigger points come, he's in control of that situation.'

●

Robert Federer gripped Roger by the back of the neck and pushed his son's head into the snowbank by the roadside. Driving along an alpine pass as they

▲ Federer as a child on court in Basel.

returned from a junior tournament, and with Roger raging and red-lining in the passenger seat about how he had played that day, Robert had stopped the car, jumped out and told the teenager to step out. How better to cool the fieriest of junior tennis hotheads than to immerse him in the snow? That was the winter day Federer's father reached the limits of his patience with his son's behaviour, and all that chuntering, cussing, screaming and bouncing of rackets. 'Can you please stop?' Robert Federer would frequently find himself calling out at his son. To which Roger would respond: 'Why don't you go and have a drink and leave me alone?' As a boy, and then as a teenager, it often felt to Federer that tennis was eating him up from the inside.

Federer may have been prone to red-hot rages, but it is not accurate to characterise his younger incarnation as the mini-McEnroe of suburban Basel. Unlike John McEnroe, whose anger was aimed at others, and in particular umpires, Federer's rage was primarily directed at himself. Federer was forever squabbling internally. From a young age, he felt it should be possible to achieve perfection on a tennis court. He once admitted to a fear of spiders, snakes, skydiving and rollercoaster rides. But what he really abhorred was imperfection, and that included those times when he won the point but was not happy with the shots he played.

In years to come, when he was a multiple Grand Slam champion who had learned how to control his emotions, Federer would be amused when someone else 'lost it'. In those moments he would recognise his old self. The way Federer remembers it, he could be 'a crazy maniac', his behaviour 'horrible'. He knew that at the time, but could not stop himself. 'I was throwing my racket around like you can't imagine,' Federer has said. 'I mean, I was getting kicked out of practice sessions. I used to talk much more, too, and scream on court.' Federer's parents threatened to stop driving him to tournaments. They told him they were

FEDERER WAS THREE YEARS OLD WHEN HE SWUNG A RACKET FOR THE FIRST TIME, AND BY THE TIME HE WAS FOUR HE COULD PLAY AS MANY AS THIRTY SHOTS IN A ROW WITHOUT MISSING.

embarrassed to be seen with him. Some of his more outrageous moments came when playing in front of a crowd. 'Is it really such a catastrophe,' his mother Lynette once asked him, 'if you lose a tennis match?' The answer was undeniably 'yes'. Many a tear was shed over a lost match. One of his first coaches, Madeleine Bärlocher, tells a story about how 'a little Roger, after losing a match, would hide behind the umpire's chair and wouldn't stop crying for more than ten minutes'. Indeed, if you visit the Old Boys Tennis Club in Basel, and stand on the Roger Federer Court, named in his honour, you can almost hear the anger – the staccato bursts of Swiss–German and the thwat-crack, thwat-crack of endangered racket frames – that was once the soundtrack to his tennis.

Born on 8 August 1981, Federer was three years old when he swung a racket for the first time. By the time he was four he could play as many as thirty shots in a row without missing. An image from the Federer family album captures Roger as a young boy with a wooden racket on a clay court – even then he had excellent technique on his forehand. Federer's introduction to the game was at a private sports club in Basel, where membership was a perk for those, like his parents, who were employed by the pharmaceutical company Ciba. Their work had brought the couple together when Robert was relocated for a few years to South Africa. There he started a relationship with a secretary in the office, Lynette Durand, after meeting her in the canteen. Robert and Lynette would play tennis on their dates after he introduced her to the sport. Both turned out to be decent club players, with Lynette the more talented of the two. On returning to Switzerland, marrying and becoming parents, it was inevitable that their two children – their eldest Diana and also Roger – would be exposed to the sport. 'My husband and I spent our weekends at the club, and Roger just picked up the racket,' Lynette said. 'We played with him on the court whenever we could.'

Somehow, it is good to hear how the greatest figure the sport has ever known worked on his game in the most clichéd, commonplace way imaginable: he would spend entire afternoons hitting the ball against the garage wall or the kitchen cupboards of their home in the middle-class suburb of Münchenstein. As Federer has recalled: 'Mum got fed up because it was bang, bang, bang all day.' Sometimes, when those games were inside, there would be breakages. When Federer was not playing tennis, he would often amuse himself by teasing his sister. 'Roger would always come around

FASTEST SERVES

RAFA NADAL

135mph/217kph (2010 US Open)

ROGER FEDERER

136mph/218kph (2007 French Open)

NOVAK DJOKOVIC

137mph/220kph (2007 Indian Wells)

ANDY MURRAY

139mph/223kph (2011 Cincinnati)

SAM GROTH – WORLD RECORD FOR THE FASTEST SERVE

163mph/262kph

50mph   100mph

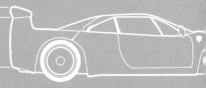

217mph/349kph
Top speed reached by Ferrari

FEDERER'S FIRST APPEARANCE IN A TOURNAMENT WAS NOT THE TRIUMPH HE MIGHT HAVE DREAMED IT WOULD BE: HE LOST 6-0, 6-0, A SCORELINE KNOWN IN SWITZERLAND AS A BICYCLE.

shouting when I was with my friends, or he would pick up the receiver when I was on the phone,' Diana once said. 'He really was a little devil.'

On the tennis court, he was an ambitious little devil. At the age of eight, Federer started playing at the Old Boys Tennis Club. At first it was in a group under the guidance of Bärlocher, but soon he was having some private lessons with another coach, Czech Seppli Kacovsky. 'Roger didn't always concentrate during the sessions,' Kacovsky said. 'Sometimes he would hit some shots and then shout, "Whack! Pow! With this shot I win Wimbledon!" Some of those balls would hit the back fence without bouncing first. He would tell me he was going to be the world number one. A lot of other kids would also say they had those same dreams, but it was like Roger was born with a racket in his hand. He had such natural talent. In all my years of coaching I had never seen such a gifted player. I could tell him how to hit a shot and he would get it straight away, while some kids might take several hours. Roger was exceptional even then.'

Federer's first appearance in a tournament was not the triumph he might have dreamed it would be: he lost 6-0, 6-0, a scoreline known in Switzerland as a bicycle. Federer was around ten years old at the time, playing against an opponent three years his senior, Reto Schmidli, who would go on to become a traffic cop in the city. It remains the only time Federer has failed to win a game in a best-of-three-set match. Looking back on that day, there are two conflicting voices in Schmidli's head, and they constantly bicker with each other. 'One tells me, "Oh, don't be stupid. He was young, just a little boy, and you were older. Come on, Reto, it was nothing". Maybe I was just lucky to have been his opponent that day, as I think that any thirteen year old would have beaten him,' Schmidli said. 'But then there's this other voice which says, "Yeah, but it was Roger Federer, and you didn't just beat him, you beat him 6-0, 6-0". It was the day I sent Roger home on his bicycle.'

There were inevitably tears then, just as there were on the hugely emotional occasion he played a close friend, Marco Chiudinelli. Every time one of them fell behind in the match, that boy would cry, to be comforted by his pal during the changeover. Another swing in momentum and they would change roles. The boy who had been doing the comforting would now be sobbing, while the other would have dried his eyes and would now have his

▲ Federer won the Orange Bowl junior tournament in Miami – and also returned home with a 250-dollar head of bleached hair.

arm around his friend's shoulder. There was some laughter among the tears, though, with Federer's humour apparent from an early age. Once, when he was due on court, he thought it would be amusing to climb a nearby tree and hide in the branches. From up there he had an excellent view of the chaos and confusion beneath as the coaches and other boys searched for him. 'Roger would laugh so loud,' Bärlocher said. 'That was one of his favourite jokes.' Still, it was a tennis education remembered as much, if not more, for tears of frustration rather than tears of mirth. Fortunately for Federer – and for the future of men's tennis – he was not discouraged, and every afternoon after school he would cycle to the courts for a coaching session with an Australian, Peter Carter.

There was another piece of good fortune. In a sport scarred by pushy parents – only stage mothers have a worse reputation – Robert and Lynette Federer were not another pair of exploiters, coercing their son to achieve any unfulfilled dreams they might have had. Far from it. During his childhood Federer did not concentrate on tennis by cutting everything else from his life; he played football and other sports, and had piano lessons. He also still attended regular school, although a teacher at his primary school, Schulhaus Neue Welt (the New World School), said he had not been the most conscientious of students. Theresa Fischbacher remembered: 'The problem was that Roger was in a classroom with a good view, so it was always tempting to look out of the window and start daydreaming.'

One of the fastest ways to blur, and then damage, the relationship between a parent and a child is for the mother or father to coach their tennis prodigy. That was never a serious issue for Robert and Lynette Federer. Almost every time Robert tried to pass on some tennis instruction, his son would not even look at him. Lynette, meanwhile, did not feel she had the patience for her son's desire to experiment rather than stick within the confines of the tennis manuals. The antithesis of the stage mother, Lynette said once that 'without the support and guidance of a parent, it will be difficult for a junior to

ACES AND DOUBLE FAULTS

Federer serves more aces from the advantage court (62 per
cent) than from the deuce court (38 per cent). He is most likely
to hit an ace down the 'T' of the advantage court (40 per cent
of all aces).

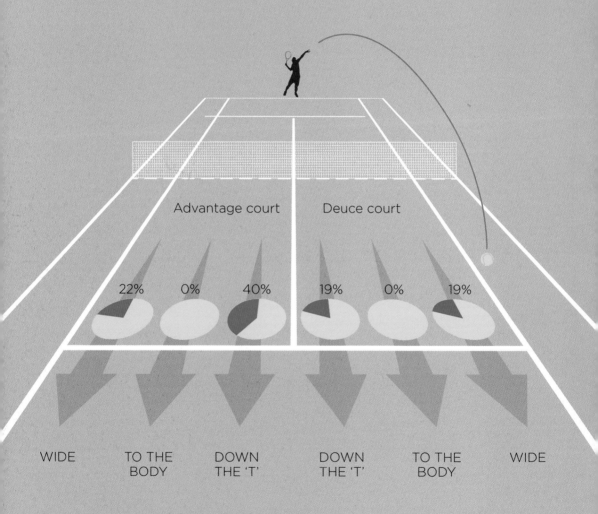

Advantage court   Deuce court

22%   0%   40%   19%   0%   19%

WIDE   TO THE   DOWN   DOWN   TO THE   WIDE
        BODY   THE 'T'   THE 'T'   BODY

ACES AND DOUBLE-FAULTS – AVERAGES PER SET IN THE GRAND SLAM FINALS FEDERER WON

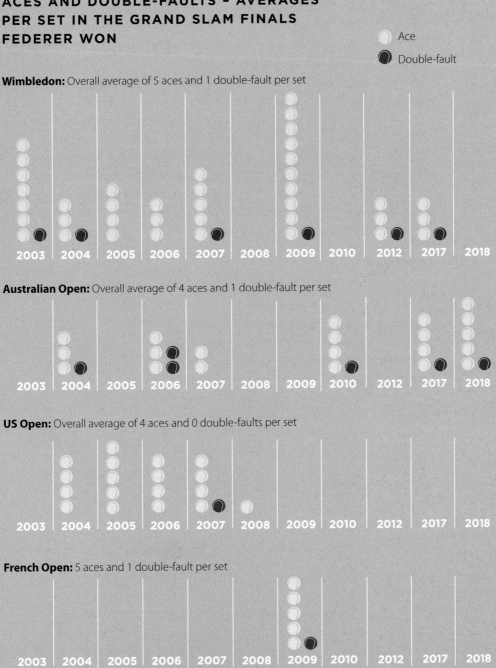

Ace

Double-fault

Wimbledon: Overall average of 5 aces and 1 double-fault per set

2003 | 2004 | 2005 | 2006 | 2007 | 2008 | 2009 | 2010 | 2012 | 2017 | 2018

Australian Open: Overall average of 4 aces and 1 double-fault per set

2003 | 2004 | 2005 | 2006 | 2007 | 2008 | 2009 | 2010 | 2012 | 2017 | 2018

US Open: Overall average of 4 aces and 0 double-faults per set

2003 | 2004 | 2005 | 2006 | 2007 | 2008 | 2009 | 2010 | 2012 | 2017 | 2018

French Open: 5 aces and 1 double-fault per set

2003 | 2004 | 2005 | 2006 | 2007 | 2008 | 2009 | 2010 | 2012 | 2017 | 2018

succeed', but that was not the same as being a pushy parent. 'I believe that parents shouldn't be too ambitious for their child. Our role as a parent of a junior tennis player is to ensure that they attend their practice, to accompany them to their matches, to motivate the child and to comfort them when necessary and, most importantly of all, to ensure that the child enjoys the game. As a parent, you shouldn't be putting pressure on the child in any way.'

More than anything, Federer's parents cared about curbing their son's rage. 'When Roger's behaviour was poor, I would say he was inviting his opponent to beat him,' Lynette said. 'We would also tell him that his behaviour was upsetting us, and used to say to him, "Come on, Roger, get control of yourself, pull yourself together".' There were two types of car journeys home from the tennis club. The ones when the family argued, the most famous being interrupted so Robert could put Roger's head into the snow. And the ones when the family sat in uncomfortable silence. In time, Lynette came to understand that her son cried because he cared so deeply. 'The tears showed how ambitious Roger was, how determined he was to succeed.'

Before Federer, Switzerland had never produced a male Grand Slam singles champion. But it is not as if the country had no history in elite tennis. After all, Marc Rosset had been an Olympic champion, as well as a Grand Slam semi-finalist, while Heinz Günthardt and Jakob Hlasek had both reached quarter-finals at the majors. From Federer's point of view, you might suggest this was ideal: other Swiss players had achieved enough in the past to maintain a tennis culture, but not so much that there would be intolerable pressure and expectation for him to emulate them. Federer had rubbed shoulders with the top players at an early age. Not far from Federer's house, at the city's St. Jakobshalle arena, an annual ATP tournament was held. His mother used to work at the event as a volunteer on the administration side. One year Federer was a ball boy. That was not the only time that a young Federer fetched balls and towels for the world elite: he also did so for Martina Hingis, the first Swiss of either sex to win a Grand Slam singles title. There is evidence of him on ball-boy duty in the shape of a fading, crumpled photograph at the Old Boys Tennis Club. 'We were very fortunate that we have a good system in Switzerland,' Lynette said. 'If a child was talented they were selected with the best of their age group and had good regional coaches. We were also lucky to have very good coaches in our local club.'

When Federer was fourteen years old, he unilaterally decided that if he

▶ Growing up, Federer was inspired by the elite players competing a short distance from his home in Basel, at the St. Jakobshalle.

was going to further his tennis career, he needed to base himself at the Swiss National Tennis Centre in Écublens on Lake Geneva. Federer did not inform his parents of this decision; instead they read about it in an interview he gave to a tennis magazine. 'We are a close family, but Roger took the decision at a very early age that he wanted to play tennis away from home. We never forced him to do anything, but let him develop on his own,' Lynette said. 'He made a lot of important decisions himself when he was younger, and that was key to his success because he had to learn how to do things for himself. He learned to be very independent.'

Even so, the move was not without its problems. Federer had difficulties with communication because Écublens was in the French-speaking part of Switzerland, and at the time he only spoke Swiss–German and English. Some of the other aspiring young players, Federer said, were 'mean'. 'I was the Swiss–German,' Federer recalled, 'who everyone liked to make fun of.' When he was not playing tennis, Federer would sit alone in his room at his host family's home, eating cereal. Federer has spoken of the 'sadness' he often felt at Écublens. On Sunday evenings, as Federer's parents drove him to the station in Basel to catch a train back to Écublens, he would usually be in tears. If his parents had imposed Écublens on him, there is a good chance he would have rebelled and refused to return. But since it had been his decision to attend, he stuck with it. His mother believes that much good came of her son's short-term struggles. 'Roger's time at Écublens was a great lesson in life for him – that things don't always go your own way, and that you don't get anywhere in life with talent alone. You have to work at things. I know that it wasn't always fun and games for Roger there, and that many days he wasn't that happy. But those struggles were good for him. Overcoming those ups and downs was a challenge for him, and it helped him to develop as a person.'

From Écublens onwards, Federer's tennis developed at quite a pace. But what did not develop at the same rate was his emotional control. After Écublens, Federer trained at a facility in Biel, and there is still an image in his head of his racket – which he had thrown – spinning through the air like a helicopter blade and then, on hitting a new curtain behind the court, slicing through the material. His punishment was a week of 7 a.m. starts, when he was made to clean the toilets and sweep the courts.

Federer's volatility was still on display when he arrived on the international tennis circuit. 'The first time I heard Roger Federer's name, I heard

FEDERER'S SERVE IN THE EIGHT WIMBLEDON FINALS HE WON

THE BIG FOUR'S SERVING DURING WIMBLEDON 2017

○ Fastest serve
● Average speed of second serve

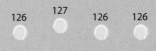

○ Fastest first serve
⌒ First serve average
● Fastest second serve
◐ Second serve average

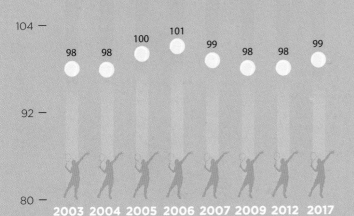

140 MPH

135

128 — 128 129 129 130 130
124 123

116 —

104 — 100 101
98   98   99   98   98   99

92 —

80 —
2003 2004 2005 2006 2007 2009 2012 2017

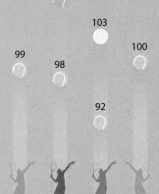

126 127 126 126

116
114 114 113 113
113 111

103
100
99   98
92

2017

Federer   Djokovic   Murray   Nadal

he had a temper,' Boris Becker said. 'I was on the phone to a friend, Peter Lundgren, and I asked him what he was doing and he said, "I'm training this unbelievable Swiss guy. He's got a temper and he's breaking rackets, but he's so good". So I thought back then that Federer was going to have to slow down with his emotions.' For a good half an hour after defeats Federer could be found in tears in the locker room. Looking back, Federer described those moments as 'a little embarrassing'.

For many years, Tim Henman said, Federer was a young man in search of his 'equilibrium'. 'When he was new to the Tour, for a while we were managed by the same person, so I got to know him pretty well. I practised with him a few times, and played against him a few times, and I thought to myself that he was potentially a top-ten player of the future and that he possibly had the game to win a Grand Slam title. He was obviously a massive talent, but he didn't yet have the right temperament or the right equilibrium,' Henman said. 'In those early years he was a little bit up and down with his practice. Some days would be good, and others days wouldn't be so good. I didn't imagine at the time that he would go on to become the greatest player who ever played the game, which is how I view him now.'

Federer was aware that he had a reputation for being soft, which was why he used a psychologist for a while. 'The word on me was "mentally, he's not the strongest"'. Occasionally his commitment was questioned. As a teenager he was accused of 'tanking', or not trying, at a small satellite tournament in Switzerland, a story that made the tabloids. And the season before he won his first Grand Slam in 2003, Federer was accused of not applying himself during an early defeat at a hard-court event in Dubai. Indeed, the tournament director initially declined to pay the player's appearance fee. Federer was extremely upset by these allegations, and returned the next year and won the title. But how was Federer supposed to behave? When he showed too much emotion he was the 'bad boy' of the courts. When he did not show enough he was said to be 'tanking'.

One way of dealing with the frustration that followed a poor practice session was to go for a drive with his then coach Peter Lundgren. The Swede would turn up the Metallica on the car stereo and encourage Federer to scream and let it all out. At night Federer would rock himself to sleep by lying on his front and butting the pillow, which he called 'head-banging'. 'What a ball of stress,' Lundgren once said of Federer.

Only a select few produce their best tennis when they are in a boiling rage. In fact, that group is so select it only contains one member: John McEnroe. Still, even McEnroe was sometimes undone by his own anger. See how he turned a two-set lead against Ivan Lendl in the 1984 French Open final into a five-set defeat after becoming upset at the noise leaking from a cameraman's headset. Eventually, almost all tennis players come to appreciate that anger is not their friend. But knowing that you need to make that change, and actually behaving differently in the white heat of competition, are two very different things. How would Federer find the emotional control needed to win Grand Slam tournaments? Ultimately, it was a tragedy – the most horrifying and devastating of news – that would change him.

10,000 ACES

During the 2017 Wimbledon Championships, Federer became only the third man, after Goran Ivanisevic and Ivo Karlovic, to hit 10,000 or more aces in his career (the ATP started collecting the data in 1991).

Average number of aces hit per match:

8

FEDERER

14

IVANIŠEVIĆ

19

KARLOVIC

2
MOZART VERSUS METALLICA

IN AN AGE OF BASELINE SLUGGERS, FEDERER'S CLASSICAL GAME IS, IN THE WORDS OF THE LATE AMERICAN AUTHOR DAVID FOSTER WALLACE, 'LIKE TRYING TO WHISTLE MOZART AT A METALLICA CONCERT'.

I t was a summer's evening in Toronto, a little before midnight, and Roger Federer was running through the city streets. He was lost, red-eyed and howling with grief. Unable to find a cab, and unsure about the way back to his hotel, he just kept running. Federer did not want to stop, maybe could not have stopped even if he had tried. He ran a mile, perhaps even a couple, before he made it back to the hotel lobby. It was a week before Federer's twenty-first birthday, and less than a year before he would win his breakthrough Grand Slam title at Wimbledon in 2003. Now he was having to confront death for the first time. That evening, Federer had been sitting in a bar, ignoring phone calls from Peter Lundgren, his then coach. While still in the doubles competition, he was already out of the singles at the hard-court tournament, and had not felt much like speaking to the Swede. But the calls had kept on coming. When Federer eventually picked up, Lundgren told him Peter Carter, his friend and coach from his younger days, had been killed while on honeymoon in South Africa.

In an age of baseline sluggers, Federer's classical game is, in the words of the late American author David Foster Wallace, 'like trying to whistle Mozart at a Metallica concert'. People forever ask how Federer came to play tennis of such majesty and beauty, and there are three answers to that question. The first: talent. The second: hard graft. The third: Peter Carter. Carter was a former professional player from the wine-making Barossa Valley north of Adelaide. His itinerant tennis life happened to bring him to the Old Boys Tennis Club in Basel after accepting an invitation to play league tennis. Without him, Roger Federer would never have truly become Roger Federer. He would not have played with such verve. He would not have embraced serve-and-volley tennis

▶ Federer is one of only four players to have won both the junior and men's Wimbledon titles.

'HE SHANKS IT HALF THE TIME, HIS SLICE SITS UP, HE TAKES A HUGE STEP WHEN HE'S OUTSIDE THE SLOT AND HE'S NOT STEPPING TO THE LEFT ON THE NEUTRAL BALL.' TO WHICH CARTER RESPONDED: 'YEAH, BUT HE'S GOING TO BE GOOD, ISN'T HE?'

to quite the same degree. He would not have had such an exquisite one-handed backhand, maybe would not even have had a single-handed backhand at all. He would not have developed a game that, years later, would become known as 'modern retro' or, if you prefer, classical with a modern twist.

Almost every part of Federer's technique can be traced back to Carter. In subsequent years Carter's parents, Bob and Diana, have taken comfort from seeing flashes of their late son's tennis in Federer's performances. Every time Federer serves and volleys, or plays a slice backhand, or displays variety, Carter's parents remember that was how Peter played the game, too. 'I can see elements of Peter's game in Roger's tennis, and I'm not the only one who says that,' Bob Carter said. 'I'm extremely proud of Peter's influence on Roger's life, and also proud of Roger, too. Peter had a great effect on Roger's tennis and character, and they were great friends. It's good to think that Roger and Peter had such a great relationship, but it's also sad as well.'

Federer was with Carter every day as a boy, and 'can't thank Peter enough for everything he did for me'. 'He wasn't my first coach, but he was my first real coach. He knew me and my game, and what was good for me,' Federer has said. Carter's own playing career had peaked at 173 in the world rankings. In all, he made a dime or two over $70,000 in prize money during the course of his tennis life (win a round or two at a Grand Slam these days and you can eclipse that in one fell swoop). Carter's old friend Darren Cahill, a fellow Australian, was bemused to learn at the time that Carter had settled in a place as slow as Basel. But it was there that Carter and Federer were introduced. Bob Carter said that Federer would have been nine or ten years old when Peter called home one day to inform them he was coaching a young boy who had the potential to become 'a very special' player.

A few years later, when Federer was thirteen years old, Cahill was in Basel to visit Carter and watched a practice session between pupil and coach. While Cahill thought that Federer had a 'fast arm, a strong forehand and a good feel for the ball', he also regarded his tennis as being far from perfect. He also thought there was an Australian contemporary, namely Lleyton Hewitt, who was showing greater promise. As Cahill would say to Carter afterwards: 'Carts, you could drive a bus through that backhand, look at that

▲ Federer with
Peter Carter, 'my
first real coach'.

thing. He shanks it half the time, his slice sits up, he takes a huge step when he's outside the slot and he's not stepping to the left on the neutral ball.' To which Carter responded: 'Yeah, but he's going to be good, isn't he?'

A good chunk of Carter's time with Federer was focused on the backhand. As a boy, Federer had felt he was almost too 'weak' to 'come over his backhand' and hit the ball flat or with topspin, and so was forced into slicing the shot. Indeed, he came to love hitting that slice. Maybe another coach would have made Federer put a second hand on the racket, and the real Roger Federer would have been lost to history. But that was not Carter's approach. Instead, he tinkered with Federer's backhand, and ensured he kept on using one hand. It was a good shot, but it was a long way from perfect, and regular upgrades and improvements would be required. Carter was teaching his young pupil more than just how to hit a backhand, though. As Federer recalled, this 'calm' coach with his 'typical Australian sense of humour' was also 'marking his character'. Years later Federer would remark that Australian traits were 'locked in my DNA'. He said: 'Work ethic was very important for

BACKHAND SPIN

Federer generates more backhand spin
than his rivals do. Figures shown are the
maximum revolutions per minute of balls
struck by the players' backhands.

Racket speed:
Revolutions per minute

FEDERER

NADAL

5,300 RPM

4,300 RPM

DJOKOVIC

2,800 RPM

MURRAY

2,500 RPM

AVERAGE 4
CYLINDER CAR

7,000 RPM

▲ Federer has
'worked a lot' on
his backhand
during his career.

Australians, so I felt I profited a lot from that early. Peter was just very important overall for my character. He taught me respect for each person. It doesn't matter whether that person was famous or not famous. He just taught me the right values, as did my parents. They got on very well. We were close to Peter, all of us.'

When the fourteen-year-old Federer started at Écublens, his association with Carter was put on pause for a couple of seasons. They would resume their player-mentor relationship at the training facility in Biel, where Federer moved from Écublens, and after the Swiss Tennis Federation hired Carter, primarily because of his close relationship with this young man of promise. It was also at Biel that Peter Lundgren, who would be in his corner for that first Wimbledon title, would become involved with Federer. In 1998, Federer excelled as a junior, winning both the Wimbledon singles and doubles titles, as well as finishing runner-up in the singles competition at the US Open, on the way to the world junior number one ranking. It was days after winning junior Wimbledon, at the age of sixteen, that Federer made his first

WHILE FEDERER WAS NOT AS FRIENDLY WITH LUNDGREN, HE CONCLUDED THAT THE SWEDE COULD DO MORE TO ACCELERATE HIS CAREER. EVEN SO, FEDERER STILL WANTED CARTER AROUND, SO MUCH SO THAT HE LOBBIED SUCCESSFULLY FOR THE AUSTRALIAN TO BECOME SWITZERLAND'S FIRST FOREIGN DAVIS CUP CAPTAIN.

appearance on the ATP World Tour. He was given a wild card into the alpine clay-court tournament in Gstaad, where he was beaten in the opening round by Argentina's Lucas Arnold Ker.

Of the four wild cards that Federer received into ATP tournaments in 1998, it was in Toulouse that he achieved his first win at that level, beating Frenchman Guillaume Raoux on the way to the quarter-finals. He also played that year against Andre Agassi in Basel, but lost heavily. The following year, Federer undertook a heavier schedule, and started to make an impression, breaking into the top 100. This was timely as his parents had informed him that they would not continue to sponsor his career if he was going to scuffle around 400 in the rankings.

Soon, Federer had to choose the coach to guide him through these first steps as a professional. Carter or Lundgren? The decision he made would astound almost everyone who knew Federer. And probably no one more than Carter, who, despite his best efforts, could not hide his deep disappointment at being overlooked. What Carter lacked was Lundgren's experience of tennis at the highest level. As a player Lundgren had been ranked inside the top twenty-five, and had defeated the likes of Pete Sampras, Andre Agassi, Mats Wilander and Ivan Lendl. As a coach he had worked with Chilean Marcelo Ríos, whose game Federer admired. It had not been an easy call for Federer to make because of his friendship with Carter. It revealed, though, that Federer would not allow personal relationships to cloud what was best for his tennis. While Federer was not as friendly with Lundgren, he concluded that the Swede could do more to accelerate his career. Even so, Federer still wanted Carter around, so much so that he lobbied successfully for the Australian to become Switzerland's first foreign Davis Cup captain.

It was Federer, with his South African mother, who had suggested his former coach should take his wife Silvia on safari. It was a belated honeymoon for the couple, who had married a year earlier, but were waiting until Silvia had completed a course of chemotherapy to combat Hodgkin's disease. On 31 July they marked Silvia's birthday. The very next day, 1 August 2002, the Carters were travelling in separate vehicles along a road near Kruger National Park. Carter was in a Land Rover, driven by a guide, with Silvia in the vehicle behind.

FOREHAND AND BACKHAND SPEED

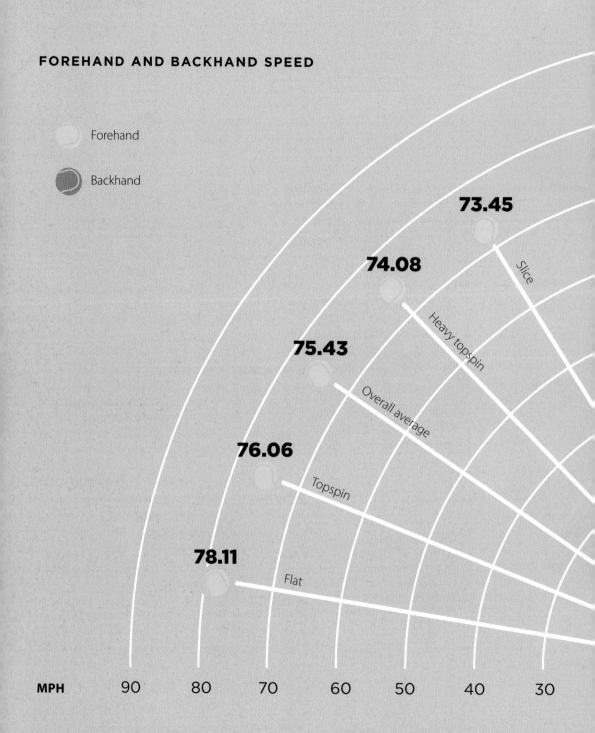

Forehand

Backhand

73.45

74.08

75.43

76.06

78.11

Slice

Heavy topspin

Overall average

Topspin

Flat

MPH   90   80   70   60   50   40   30

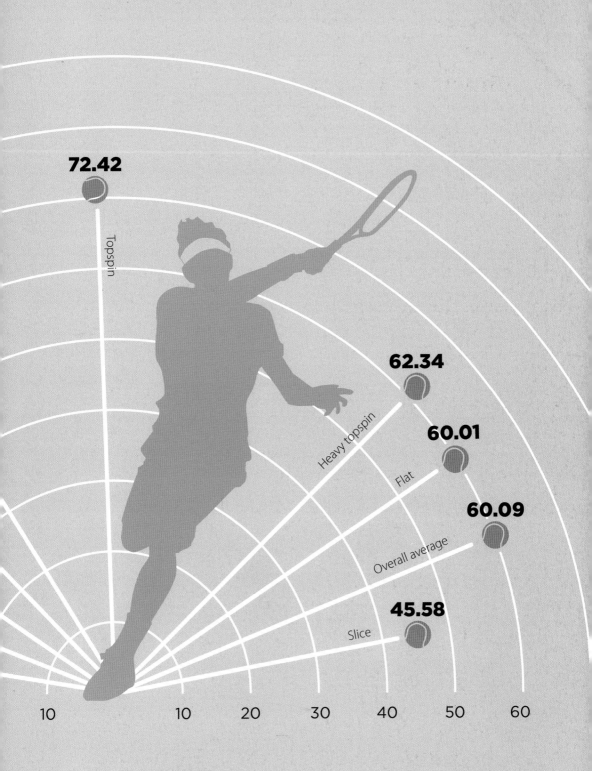

72.42

Topspin

62.34

Heavy topspin

60.01

Flat

60.09

Overall average

45.58

Slice

10 10 20 30 40 50 60

When an oncoming minibus appeared in the road, the Land Rover carrying Carter swerved to avoid a head-on collision, spun down a bank and landed upside down in a river. According to the police report, Carter and the guide were killed instantly.

For Federer, now back in his hotel room after running through the Toronto night, this was news beyond comprehension.

●

Consider what Roger Federer's single-handed backhand represents – the seemingly effortless beauty of his game, and also the sweat and the toil, and his desire for self-improvement – and this shot would appear to be the most elegant, the most glorious, of contradictions.

The galleries might care deeply about the beauty in Federer's game. Federer's own thoughts, though, have shifted over the years. In his early days on the Tour, Federer concerned himself a little too much with always playing the classiest, the most gorgeous shot. There was a danger that his matches were tipping over into trick shows, and that he was selecting the technically difficult and spectacular over the smart. He was almost as concerned with creating a highlights reel as winning the match. That did not just apply to his backhand, but to every part of his game. How many matches did he lose because he felt a pressure from the crowd to create the prettiest point they had ever seen? For a long while, according to Peter Lundgren, Federer regarded himself as 'an artist', and liked to watch his matches back on video. 'I have to admit,' Federer once said, 'that when I joined the professional tour, I liked to think I was bringing something special and I would show off.' Here is another admission: 'I really felt as though I had to please the crowd, but it made me lose.' That is no longer how he thinks about his tennis. Federer certainly likes the fact he is appreciated for his art, telling the *New Yorker* magazine: 'I play old-school tennis with my one-handed backhand and I'm happy it pleases the eye, let's put it that way.' But that does not mean Federer cares more about style than he does about winning – he does not 'purposefully try to make [my tennis] graceful or classy', he just happens to have a 'vintage style'. All that matters is how his backhand, and the rest of his game, help him to defeat his opponents. Given a choice, he would always choose the Brad Gilbert way, and winning ugly, over losing beautifully. It is only because Federer has won so much that the beauty in his game is celebrated.

It is all very well watching Federer play and feeling as though you are being transported back to the sport's sepia years, to an age of wooden rackets and flannel trousers, while also thinking that the modern game lacks art, guile and soul. But what matters is that the vintage repelled, and then quashed, and then destroyed, the modern. Federer has demonstrated how you can more than hold your own with a one-hander. Who needs a second hand on the racket? Apart from the improvised shot he played at Roland Garros in 2015, who can remember another double-handed backhand from Federer? Traditional does not have to mean soft, effete, easily pushed around.

It is when Federer is crushing an opponent that his backhand becomes ever more alluring and distracting. It distracts you from how Federer's backhand is also a metaphor for his hard graft. 'The most perfect player', John McEnroe once called Federer. Central to the Federer mythology is that he is so gifted that he has never had to work at his game, that his technique and his success have come easily to him. One French tennis writer seems to have bought into that, labelling Federer's game 'a permanent miracle'. The reality is that, to carry yourself as an aesthete and a sophisticate, you have to be a toiler.

Almost from his first appearances on the professional scene, Federer's forehand had menace, and he could also do damage with his serve and his volleys. Of course, those shots have improved and became even more potent. But those upgrades were small when set against the development of Federer's backhand, which was once described as the nearest thing he had to a weakness. Federer has said that it is a shot he has 'worked on a lot throughout my career'. Besides Peter Carter, and his other coaches, Federer also has to thank all those opponents who targeted that wing for the improvements he has made to his single-handed backhand. Players such as Rafa Nadal gave him 'a million backhands' to try and put him under extreme pressure. It is instructive to read the passage in the Spaniard's autobiography about the tactics he used against Federer in the 2008 Wimbledon final and how he would only hit to Federer's forehand if he 'lost concentration' or 'had a rush of blood to his head'. Otherwise, every ball was sent towards Federer's backhand. And that was on grass. On clay, Nadal's whippy, heavily-spun forehands would rear up and have Federer hitting his backhand just where he did not want it, above shoulder height, up around his ears.

GAP BETWEEN WINNING JUNIOR AND SENIOR TITLES AT WIMBLEDON

Federer is among a small group of players to have won both the junior and senior titles at Wimbledon.

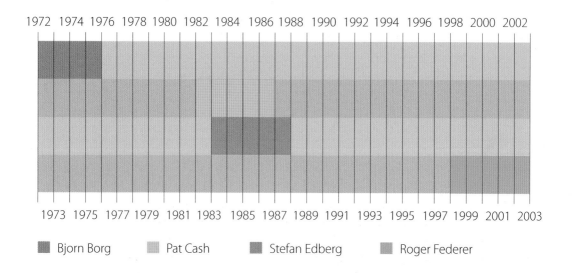

1972 1974 1976 1978 1980 1982 1984 1986 1988 1990 1992 1994 1996 1998 2000 2002

1973 1975 1977 1979 1981 1983 1985 1987 1989 1991 1993 1995 1997 1999 2001 2003

■ Bjorn Borg   ■ Pat Cash   ■ Stefan Edberg   ■ Roger Federer

Rafa Nadal's uncle and coach, Toni, looks at Federer's backhand today and recognises how the Swiss has worked hard to become a better player. 'I'm certain that Roger's backhand improved and that he adapted to how Rafael played against him,' Toni said. 'On every surface, not just on clay, but on hard courts and on grass as well, Rafael would be attacking Roger's backhands. If Rafael could hit three or four balls to Roger's backhand, more often than not the point would be Rafael's. But that was true during their first few matches. After those meetings Roger changed his way, including his position – he went further into the court – and then it was different. I'm convinced Roger thought to himself, "This isn't enough, my backhand isn't enough at the moment", and he knew that he had to improve, so that's what he did.'

Using just one hand enables Federer to be aggressive with his sliced backhand. 'Roger has the best slice in the world, especially when he is slicing on the return of serve,' said Richard Gasquet, who himself has a single-handed backhand, and who in his youth was known as 'Baby Federer'. 'The biggest difference between my backhand and Roger's is that he can play that slice.

What talent he has. The feeling he has with the ball, that's just incredible.' John Yandell, a tennis videographer and analyst, has discovered that Federer's backhand slice generates more spin – up to 90 revolutions per second – than any other shot in the sport, above even the forehands of Nadal and Federer. John McEnroe's analysis is that Federer's slice puts great uncertainty in an opponent's mind. 'He wants you to feel unsettled and to not know what is coming next.' Federer's sliced backhand has been so effective, Tim Henman has said, because it enables him to change the pace of the rally. He can slow the point down with the slice and then, from nowhere, speed it up again with a flat or topspin ball. 'And that means he makes more impact with that next shot.'

As a child, Federer took more pleasure from playing the slice than any other shot. But the older version of himself is aware that you cannot live on slices alone. Additionally, he recognises that players with a one-handed backhand must avoid the temptation of 'bailing out' and selecting the safe option of a slice when a flat or heavy topspin backhand would put an opponent at greater discomfort. One of the many reasons to admire Federer is his stubbornness when his backhand has come under attack. He does not retreat. Instead he stays just where he is, and continues to take big swings at the ball, even if he shanks a few. 'If you have a one-handed backhand,' Federer has said, 'it's so natural to play the slice that you almost have to tell yourself to stay on the front foot and be aggressive.'

Federer cannot risk the shot becoming predictable. At all times his opponent must be guessing what is coming next. 'It's important to set yourself up so that you have multiple options. That's when you are most dangerous for your opponent,' according to Federer. 'Don't always hit in the same spot. What you want to do early in the match is to show your opponent that you can hit all the shots so when it gets important in the match he doesn't know where it's going to go. I can hit the slice, the topspin and the flat backhand. I try to mix it up as much as I can. But, at the same time, I also need to be able to make enough in a row just for consistency and also for my confidence.'

Be thankful that when Federer has experimented during practice with a two-handed backhand, just to experience how most play the game, he has found it to be uncomfortable and limiting. It helped to confirm why he prefers the freedom of a one-hander. Nick Bollettieri, arguably the most successful coach in tennis history, believes that Federer would have been almost

unbeatable with a double-handed backhand. But others strongly disagree, saying that if Federer had two hands on the racket it would be at a considerable cost to his touch and variety. 'If Roger had been two-handed, he would have won fewer majors, not more,' said the analyst Craig O'Shannessy. 'You look at the greatest volleyers in the history of the game and they all have one common denominator. They have a one-handed backhand. When you come to the net to volley, the most important thing is getting the grip right. If you have a one-handed backhand, you don't have to think about your grip when you hit the first volley, and you also find it easier to get the angle of the racket right. It stays constant. OK, so he's not Agassi bashing away at his backhand from the back of the court, but Roger's backhands are so much better.'

Part of what is so fascinating about Federer's backhand is that it is the one part of his game that young players are not trying to rip off. They might try to copy his serve, his forehand and the way he glides about the court. But very rarely, if at all, do you encounter juniors who are modelling their backhand on Federer's one-handed version. It is the double-hander every time. 'It's a little surprising,' admitted Gasquet. 'But as a junior when you want to play well and to improve your game, it's easier to have a two-hander. With a one-handed backhand, it's more aesthetic and you're able to play with more feeling. Of course, the one-handed backhand will disappear. I can't think of one very good young player on the way up who has a one-handed backhand.'

As Federer says, the single-handed backhand isn't the future.

●

Up until he took that call from Peter Lundgren informing him that Peter Carter had been killed, Roger Federer had avoided death and grief. He had never lost anyone close to him. He had never been to a funeral. That ghastly night in Toronto, Federer returned to his hotel room and called friends to pass on the news. One person who spoke to Federer then would later say that he had sounded 'destroyed' down the line.

One theory about how Federer learned to take control of his on-court emotions is that his outlook was turned around by a wild night in Rome involving Marat Safin, some busted rackets and an Italian television network. On leaving the clay court at the Foro Italico after a second-round match at the

◀ Federer prefers the freedom of a one-handed backhand.

1ST MATCH ON THE ATP WORLD TOUR IN 1998: FEDERER APPEARED AS A WILD CARD IN A CLAY-COURT TOURNAMENT IN GSTAAD, AND LOST IN STRAIGHT SETS TO ARGENTINA'S LUCAS ARNOLD KER

1ST FINAL RUNNER-UP TO SWITZERLAND'S MARC ROSSET AT AN INDOOR HARD-COURT TOURNAMENT IN MARSEILLE IN 2000

1ST TITLE DEFEATED FRENCHMAN JULIEN BOUTTER IN THE FINAL OF AN INDOOR CARPET TOURNAMENT IN MILAN IN 2001

▲ Federer has always enjoyed playing a sliced backhand.

2001 tournament, with his endorphin and adrenaline levels still high, Federer returned to the locker room. The television was on. Expecting the Italian network to be discussing how he had won a final-set tiebreak, Federer was surprised to hear that the analysis was focusing instead on the orgy of racket-smashing during the match. That surprise soon turned to embarrassment. Replays showed Federer and Safin laying waste to their equipment. In that moment Federer told himself he had to bring all this rage and violence to an end. That is one theory, anyway. A much more persuasive analysis is that it was the tragedy of Carter's death which transformed his approach to tennis.

In the short term Federer's tennis collapsed. Wearing a black armband, Federer went ahead and played a doubles match in Toronto alongside South Africa's Wayne Ferreira. It was hardly surprising that they lost that quarter-final to the Australian pair Joshua Eagle and Sandon Stolle. Already that summer Federer's singles form had been disappointing: he had lost on his opening appearances at Roland Garros, Wimbledon and Toronto. He suffered similar results in the two tournaments that followed Carter's passing, with early defeats in Cincinnati and Long Island. At once Federer could see how trivial tennis was, but he also suddenly had clarity on how he would have to dedicate his life to the sport if he was to make the most of his talent. 'It was the first death Roger had to deal with and it was a deep shock for him,' his

'THE SHOTS HE COMES UP WITH IN CERTAIN SITUATIONS, THEY ARE JUST AMAZING. SOME OF THEM, YOU CAN'T BELIEVE THAT HE CAN PRODUCE THOSE SORTS OF SHOTS WHEN HE IS UNDER SO MUCH PRESSURE. BUT HE DOES IT, TIME AND TIME AGAIN, AND THAT'S HIM. HE'S PROBABLY THE BIGGEST TALENT WHO HAS EVER PLAYED THIS GAME.'

mother, Lynette, said. 'But it also made him stronger.'

An Australian mourner at Carter's funeral in Basel reported: 'Roger was utterly inconsolable, crying before, during and after the service, which was an incredibly sad occasion. I remember standing in a group, which included Roger, and we all ended up laughing with Roger about his lack of emotional control.' Federer admitted afterwards: 'Any defeat in tennis is nothing compared to such a moment. I usually try to avoid sad moments like this, and it was the first time I'd been to a funeral. I can't say that it did me any good, but I was very close to him in thought once again, and I could say goodbye in a dignified setting. I feel somewhat better now, especially in matters concerning tennis.'

In time, those around Federer noticed a change in him, and he would qualify for the 2002 season-ending tournament, the first time he had been among that group of eight elite players. 'When Peter died, it was a wake-up call for Roger,' Bob Carter said. 'I think he realised that if he was to become a top player, he would have to calm down on the court.'

The next summer Federer won his first Grand Slam title, and Carter was in his thoughts. 'I guess we would have had a big party if Peter had been here. I hope he saw it from somewhere.' Just a few weeks later, Switzerland and Australia met in a Davis Cup tie in Melbourne. On the court the tie is remembered for Federer failing to close out a winning position in a singles rubber against Lleyton Hewitt. Off the court there was a more significant meeting: between Federer and Carter's parents. They sat and shared stories about Peter. At one point Bob turned to Federer and said: 'Roger, just do the best you can, mate. Peter thought the world of you. He thought you might be something pretty special.' Every year Federer invites Carter's parents to be his guests at the Australian Open. 'Roger pays for our flights, the hotel room, a car, the whole works,' Bob said. 'And we sit in his box during matches.' Between matches, they reminisce.

Stefan Edberg, who coached Federer from 2014 for two years, was known during his playing career for his cool approach to the most heated of situations. The Swede believes it is often necessary for a tennis player to 'train his mind'. 'Sometimes it takes time to change your approach on court. Roger used to be more emotional on court and he taught himself to be calmer. As you get older, you realise that tennis is more complicated – there are so many elements that go into it – and that the mind is so important.'

Such is Federer's emotional control now that it can be difficult to imagine a time when he used to be a 'crazy maniac'. 'Mentally, Roger used to have a big problem, but he has become so brilliant at dealing with pressure,' said Goran Ivanišević, a former Wimbledon champion. 'The shots he comes up with in certain situations, they are just amazing. Some of them, you can't believe that he can produce those sorts of shots when he is under so much pressure. But he does it, time and time again, and that's him. He's probably the biggest talent who has ever played this game, and he has proved that time and time again. But to use that talent he first had to work on his mind and become mentally stronger.'

These days John McEnroe speaks of Federer being 'painfully relaxed', while Jimmy Connors sometimes wonders whether the Swiss 'even has a pulse'. Pop into the locker room five minutes before a Wimbledon final, Andy Roddick has observed, and Federer is as calm as if he were about to play a practice match during the close season. That emotional control continues after walking on to Centre Court. And even if Federer loses, he is able to process that setback at rapid speed. Mary Carillo, a former player and now a broadcaster, once spoke of Federer being 'pathologically optimistic'. One of his former coaches, José Higueras, agreed. 'One of the things that impressed me was how he could move on quickly after a defeat. After the 2008 French Open final, when Roger won just four games against Nadal, I think I was more upset than Roger was. I also felt bad for Roger after he lost that year's Wimbledon final to Nadal. But Roger was facing Nadal at his peak that summer, and he didn't dwell on those defeats – later that summer, he would win the US Open.'

So Federer became the most urbane of tennis players, the calmest and coolest figure in tennis since the unflappable ice man Bjorn Borg. But that is not to say that, at the end of his fire-to-ice transformation, Federer now plays tennis with a blank mind, utterly devoid of feeling or emotion. He does not have a cauterised soul. And neither should he be oversimplified or sanitised. He is far too complicated and interesting for that. Federer's great accomplishment has not been that he has managed to turn off all his emotions, but that he has trained himself to control those emotions. The rage

▶ Only very rarely does Federer now show emotion during matches.

is still there, but it is buried deep.

Occasionally, it is necessary to be reminded that Federer still has emotions, and still has to contend with the psychological challenges of playing tennis, like everyone else. Sometimes, those reminders are on the court – with his tears and multilingual exhortations of 'Chum jetzt', 'C'mon' or 'Allez' – but sometimes off the court, with his headbanging into hotel pillows. And the night he experienced his 'Tokyo Terrors'. One of the most terrifying experiences of Federer's tennis life came when he awoke, scared and confused, in a Japanese hotel room. 'I must have had a nightmare. I jumped out of bed and stood up screaming in a state of shock. I didn't know where I was and I ran back and hit the corner of my bed, which was solid wood and sharp. Luckily, Mirka was there. She had woken up because of all the noise I was making. She turned the light on, grabbed me and told me to relax,' Federer disclosed. 'I don't know what would have happened if Mirka hadn't been there. It was pretty scary for a moment. It had never happened to me before and I hope it will never happen again.'

There was some disagreement between Federer and Mirka, then his girlfriend, now his wife and mother of their children, over the cause of the nightmare. Federer thought it had been brought on by drinking a sake bomber at dinner. Mirka believed that Federer's mind had been unsettled by playing too much tennis. The inclination is to side with Mirka and discount the local cocktail. The tale reveals much about the pressures that afflict modern tennis players. That 2 a.m. episode in Tokyo came during Federer's peak years, from 2004 to 2007, when he was about as unbeatable as any tennis player has been. Yet the expectation built and built until he had a name for it: 'The Monster.' It is incredible how Federer has managed to tame the beast.

However, Federer's old adversaries offer reminders of how the Swiss feels emotions just like everyone else. And of his combative, competitive spirit. He can dance, he can also fight. 'Just because we think that Federer isn't a street-fighter or a rip-your-head-off guy, that doesn't mean it's not in there,' said Andy Roddick. 'You don't win all those Grand Slams without having that burning desire.'

Looking at photographs of the prize-giving ceremonies at the Grand Slams over the past decade or so, it might appear that Federer is the most emotional man in tennis, not the least. While Federer sometimes cries at the cinema or theatre – he sobbed when watching the Broadway show *Finding*

▲ Federer, pictured here after winning Wimbledon for the first time, can become very emotional after his victories.

Neverland with his family during the 2015 US Open – it is tennis that makes him shake with emotion. The morning after winning his first Grand Slam title, Federer was having breakfast at the house he had rented in Wimbledon Village. As he scanned through a selection of British newspapers, he saw that there were more images of him in tears than of him holding up the golden trophy. When Federer returned to Basel and ran into Madeleine Bärlocher, one of his former coaches, she said to him: 'You used to cry after you lost matches, and now you cry after winning matches.' On teary occasions like that afternoon on Centre Court, Federer does not want to cry. He is aware of how this might look for 'the millions of people watching on television'. But he just cannot help himself. These might be happy tears, but they are also tears of relief, that all the effort has paid off.

Another highly emotional occasion was when he won the 2006 Australian Open and was presented with the trophy by the legendary Rod Laver. Tears have also flowed in defeat, such as in the aftermath of losing the 2009 Australian Open final to Rafa Nadal. 'God, it's killing me,' he told the crowd in the Rod Laver Arena after breaking down during the speeches, and Nadal consoling him. On finishing runner-up to Novak Djokovic at the 2014 Wimbledon Championships, a single tear rolled down his cheek.

When the match is over, Federer is not afraid to emote. When the contest is still live, Federer is more than capable of controlling himself. He will not allow emotions to take hold of him. He is never going to bloody his knuckles by punching his strings, as Andy Murray has, or rant at his guests' box, as both Murray and Djokovic have. Very rarely will you see the Roger of old resurface. One occasion was at a tournament in Miami in 2009, during a semi-final against Djokovic, when Federer whacked the racket on the hard court, and then tossed the broken frame towards his chair. Tennis player destroys racket, nothing remarkable to see here. This breakage, though, made the news around the world.

3
LE PETIT PETE

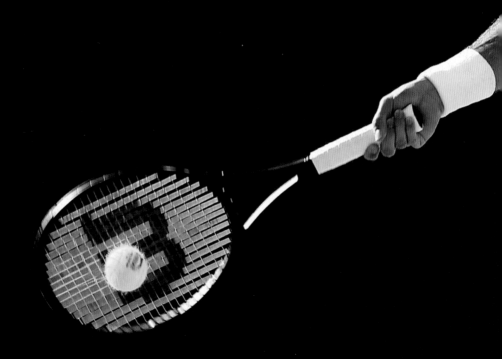

'HE CAN HIT THE BALL LOW OR HIGH, AND HE CAN PLAY WITH SPIN OR FLAT. WHAT MAKES HIS FOREHAND SO DANGEROUS IS THAT HE CAN PRODUCE A WINNER FROM ANYWHERE ON THE COURT. THERE'S NOWHERE WHERE YOU THINK YOU'RE SAFE.'

'When Roger is hitting his forehand well, you just can't breathe,' Richard Gasquet said. 'He takes the ball early and boom, boom, boom, you have no time against him. Boom, boom, boom, the forehands keep on coming. Boom, boom, boom, Roger just keeps on pushing you with his forehand. He doesn't stop.' Pete Sampras, meanwhile, describes Federer's forehand as 'the greatest shot in the game over the past ten years or so'. 'It's especially wicked when Roger takes control of a point,' Sampras said. 'He hits the forehand hard, with pace and spin. He can flatten it out when he wants to. It's just a shot that he has so much confidence in, as he should do. He has always had great technique, and he took that and developed it into a great shot.'

The sound of a Federer forehand is distinctive. Such is the blend of power and spin, that his forehand sounds like no other. There is also the variety. The videographer John Yandell has identified at least twenty-seven different forehands that Federer hits, which is considerably more than any other player. Toni Nadal, Rafa's coach, believes that Federer's forehand is 'the best in the world', even better than his nephew's. 'Roger has very high control with his forehand. He can hit the ball low or high, and he can play with spin or flat. What makes his forehand so dangerous is that he can produce a winner from anywhere on the court. There's nowhere where you think you're safe.'

But that variety has not always been so helpful to Federer's cause. As a young man Federer was bewildered by choice. While more limited players had a strong idea of which shot to play at any given moment, Federer had so many different strokes to choose from that it became tricky to decide. When a slow ball came over the net he was mentally flicking through the catalogue. 'My

▶ Pete Sampras has said that Federer has a 'wicked' forehand.

range of shots was a problem. You get a slow ball and you think, "What am I going to do with this?" If your game is limited, it's simple and you have a shot for every situation and you play it. I had too many options and I had to learn to choose the right shots and the right tactics,' he explained. As John McEnroe noted, Federer had so many options that he 'confused himself'. What Federer needed was some order, structure and rhythm to his game. Just as he runs patterns for his serve, he does the same for the rest of his tennis.

There are three reasons, the analyst Craig O'Shannessy said, why Federer runs around his backhand to play a forehand. 'Firstly, he's upgrading from a backhand to a forehand and a lot of it is about miles an hour. It's just a bigger shot, and one which can do damage to an opponent's psyche. You're saying to your opponent, "Let me put this pistol down and grab a rifle". The second reason is that Federer doubles his target area. 'You're opening up the court and so have much more court to aim at,' O'Shannessy said. 'Thirdly, Roger has complete disguise. I've looked at some of Roger's run-around forehands frame by frame, and the opponent was split-stepping up and down as he had no clue where the ball was going. Even as the racket is approaching the ball you don't know. The opponent's reaction time is taken away.'

Most tennis players, argued O'Shannessy, fall for the illusion of the open court. Time after time they will go too early for what looks like an open court, not appreciating that their opponent will cover. Federer, though, likes to hit behind his opponent, and it is a strategy that destabilises the man on the other side of the net. 'From studying Roger for years, and in particular in slow-motion, the more I saw he was playing behind opponents. That court looks open, but the ball takes one and a bit seconds to get there, and the opponent covers

◀ Federer practises his forehand while being watched by his then coach Peter Lundgren.

FOREHAND SPIN

Racket speed: revolutions per second

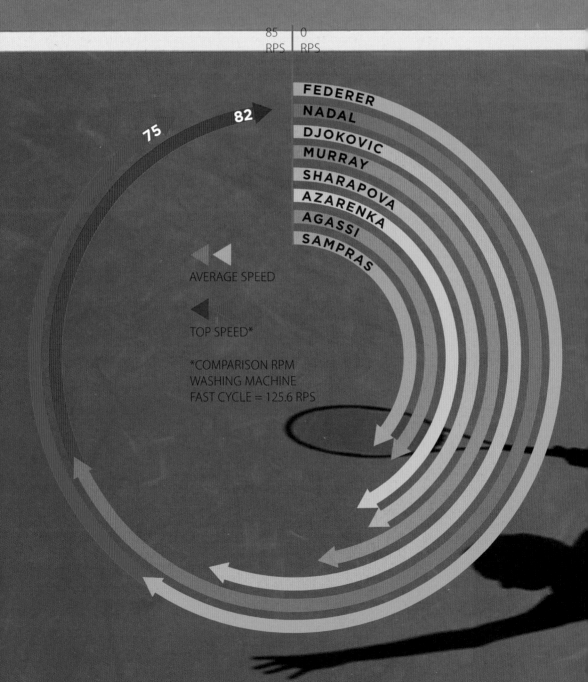

85 RPS

0 RPS

75   82

FEDERER
NADAL
DJOKOVIC
MURRAY
SHARAPOVA
AZARENKA
AGASSI
SAMPRAS

AVERAGE SPEED

TOP SPEED*

*COMPARISON RPM
WASHING MACHINE
FAST CYCLE = 125.6 RPS

YOUNG, CRAZY AND
WILD. PONYTAILED, TOO.
IT COULD DESCRIBE A
REGULAR IN BASEL'S
DIVE-BARS. BUT IT IS
ROGER FEDERER'S
DESCRIPTION OF HOW
HE WAS AS A NINETEEN
YEAR OLD AT THE
2001 WIMBLEDON
CHAMPIONSHIPS

that. Roger takes a different approach. His opponent might be standing very close to where Roger is hitting the ball, but the opponent has to stop, he has to move a couple of steps, and he has to get reorganised, and he has to get his hands and his feet set. That's tough.'

By playing the first two or three shots, sometimes more, behind his opponent Federer opens up a giant hole on the other side of the court, and this open court is not an illusion. 'There are certain times when Federer uses his forehand to attack an opponent's forehand, but in general there's no real benefit. You will see that most of Roger's forehands go to the opponent's backhand, but then most of his forehand winners go to the hole,' O'Shannessy said. One strategy that Federer sometimes employs is throwing his opponent in a 'backhand cage'. 'Roger hits four, five forehands to the opponent's backhand. And who in tennis can hit that number of backhands against Roger's forehand? Roger is saying to the other guy, "I'm putting you in the cage and you're not coming out of it".'

As Gasquet said, boom, boom, boom, the forehands keep on coming.

●

Young, crazy and wild. Ponytailed, too. It could describe a regular in Basel's dive-bars (if indeed such places even exist in that city). But it is Roger Federer's description of how he was as a nineteen year old at the 2001 Wimbledon Championships, the tournament at which he announced himself as a champion of the future. Federer had great affection for an opponent who had won a record seven Wimbledon titles, and who was on a thirty-one-match undefeated streak at the All England Club. 'I remember when the draw came out, I thought to myself, "Oh God, I could play Pete [Sampras] in the fourth round". That was a little stressful for me. It was a nice stress, though,' Federer said. 'It was my first appearance on Centre Court and I was going to play against one of my heroes.'

In the tennis talking shop, people are forever debating how matches between legends from different generations would have played out. With Federer and Sampras there is no need to wonder as it really happened, though it was a long way from a meeting of two athletes at their peaks. Though

FOREHAND AND BACKHAND

Does Federer hit more winners with his forehand or backhand?
And which shot produces more unforced errors?

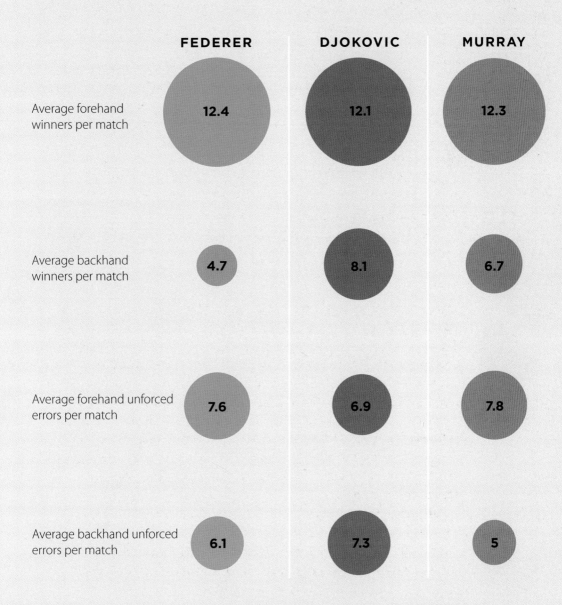

	FEDERER	DJOKOVIC	MURRAY
Average forehand winners per match	12.4	12.1	12.3
Average backhand winners per match	4.7	8.1	6.7
Average forehand unforced errors per match	7.6	6.9	7.8
Average backhand unforced errors per match	6.1	7.3	5

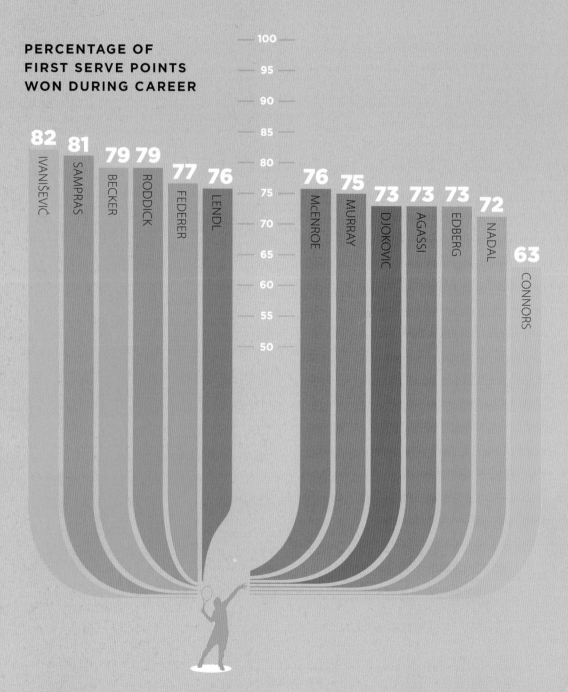

PERCENTAGE OF
FIRST SERVE POINTS
WON DURING CAREER

82 IVANIŠEVIĆ
81 SAMPRAS
79 BECKER
79 RODDICK
77 FEDERER
76 LENDL
76 McENROE
75 MURRAY
73 DJOKOVIC
73 AGASSI
73 EDBERG
72 NADAL
63 CONNORS

100
95
90
85
80
75
70
65
60
55
50

Sampras still had a Grand Slam in him – he would win the following year's US Open to take his collection of majors to what was then a record fourteen – he was not at his best. And neither was Federer, who was still a work in progress. Another of Federer's idols, Boris Becker, was inside a television commentary booth that day, calling what has turned out to be the most picked-over last-sixteen match in Grand Slam history. 'Up close, sitting in that box, I watched Federer play for the first time and thought to myself, "Wow"', Becker said.

In his youth, Federer was given the nickname 'Le Petit Pete'. Both he and Sampras had superb serves and could do damage with their forehands, though they may not stand up to comparison now as there are many more dimensions to Federer's tennis. Sampras, who would never win another Wimbledon title, regards that Centre Court match as 'the beginning for Roger'. 'That day I felt as though Roger was on the verge of greatness,' Sampras said. 'From my standpoint that was a disappointing loss, but Roger played well to win that day. He already had all the shots and it was just a case of pulling it all together. When I look back, I can see that it was a changing of the guard. It took him a couple of years after that match for him to figure out his game, and to get even better. His victory against me was a sign of things to come. We saw all the shots. We saw that he could serve well, and move well, and that he could do everything well. Who knew where it was going to go from there? It took him a little while to settle into his game and to become the best player in the world. It was a matter of becoming tougher mentally, and of physically being in great shape, and once he had it figured out, there was no stopping him.' The five-set victory took him into the quarter-finals for the first time, where he lost to Britain's Tim Henman, though that may in part have been down to injury.

After the American's retirement, Sampras and Federer became close. Sampras sent several text messages to Federer, and also called to congratulate him on winning the 2006 US Open. The next spring, Federer contacted Sampras before heading to the hard-court tournament at California's Indian Wells Tennis Garden and suggested they meet up in Los Angeles for a practice session or two. Sampras readily agreed and the two hit some balls in Sampras's back garden. 'We had a hit for a few hours, played a few points, did some drills and spoke about tennis, about the different generations,' said Sampras. But it was later that year, during an off-season mini-tour of Asian cities, that the two grew close. On one of the first nights of that tour, Federer said to Sampras: 'Let's go out for dinner, let's hang out.' That, according to Sampras, was when the friendship really began. 'I didn't know Roger that well before then, and on the first day we were a bit shy with each other, and didn't really know how to act around each other. But once we got past that it was great, and we realised our personalities are similar.'

Not completely similar, though. 'Roger is a bit of a prankster. That's a side of him that a lot of people don't see. Roger's obviously very serious on the court, and when he walks into a TV studio or press conference he still has his game face on, but once the cameras and the microphones are off Roger is very light-hearted. He loves practical jokes and he loves laughing. I've always found him very easy to be around and an all-round good guy. I remember when we were travelling in Asia on tour, I thought to myself, "This guy is like he's in high school". I'm slightly embarrassed to be telling you this, but he would come up and blow in your ear or scream in your ear. That's sort of a silly story, but it tells you about his light-hearted attitude, and how he's a down-to-earth guy. It's become a good friendship.'

It is also an important relationship for Federer. Who else but Sampras can truly relate to how Federer thinks about tennis? And how he might be feeling, and how he might be experiencing the sport? Before Federer it was Sampras who held the records for the most Grand Slam singles titles and the greatest number of weeks spent at number one. Why, the two even have a coach in common in Paul Annacone. On another trip to Los Angeles, Federer went for dinner with Sampras and then the pair went to watch the L.A. Lakers. 'It was just two guys hanging out at a basketball game,' Sampras said, 'and I think it

PERCENTAGE OF SECOND SERVE POINTS WON DURING CAREER – ALL SURFACES

PERCENTAGE OF SERVICE GAMES WON – ALL SURFACES

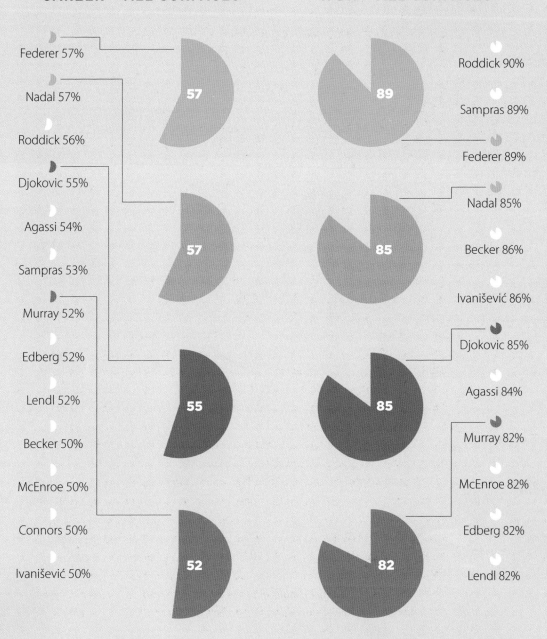

Federer 57%

Nadal 57%

Roddick 56%

Djokovic 55%

Agassi 54%

Sampras 53%

Murray 52%

Edberg 52%

Lendl 52%

Becker 50%

McEnroe 50%

Connors 50%

Ivanišević 50%

57

57

55

52

Roddick 90%

Sampras 89%

Federer 89%

Nadal 85%

Becker 86%

Ivanišević 86%

Djokovic 85%

Agassi 84%

Murray 82%

McEnroe 82%

Edberg 82%

Lendl 82%

89

85

85

82

TIEBREAKS

Federer has one of the highest winning percentages in the ATP's history.

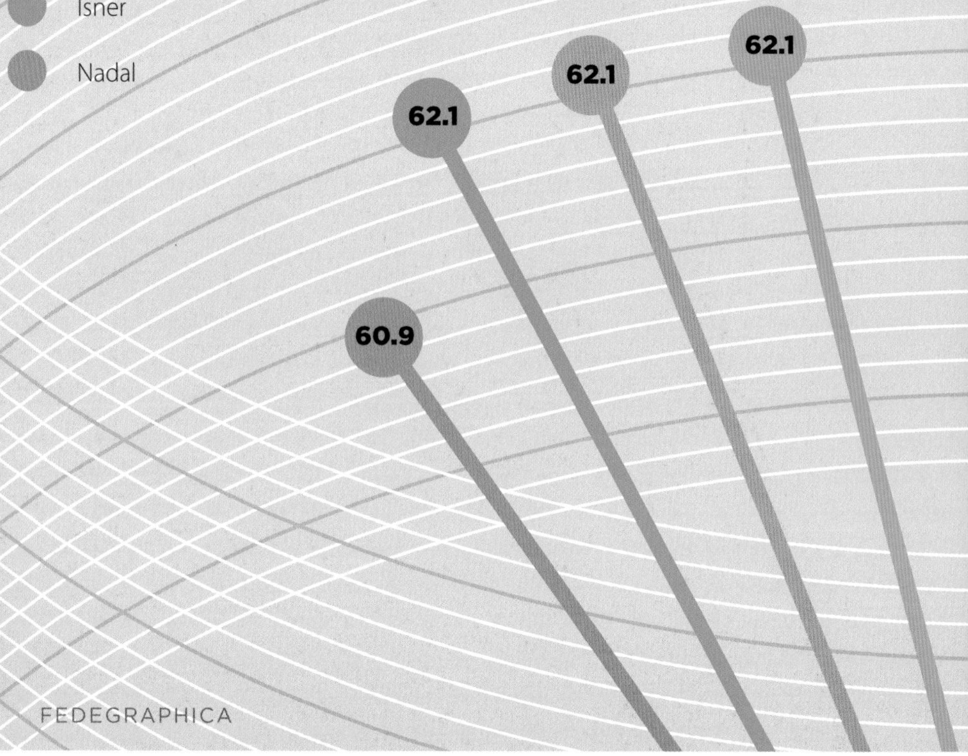

- Cash
- Federer
- Sampras
- Djokovic
- Murray
- Roddick
- Isner
- Nadal

60.9

62.1

62.1

62.1

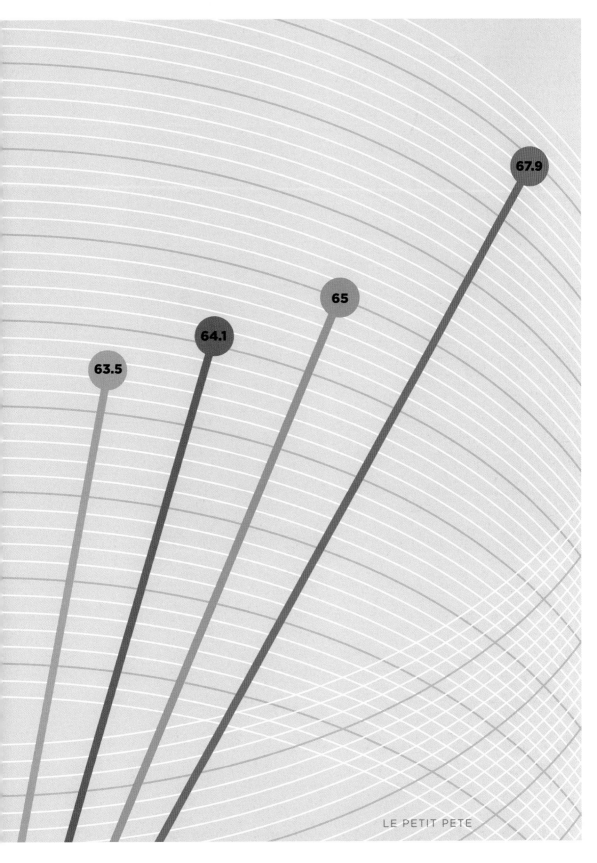

LE PETIT PETE

▲ Sampras
regards his defeat
to Federer as 'the
beginning for
Roger.'

was good for him just to get away from tennis for a bit.' About the only time there has been any awkwardness between the two men came when Sampras brought up the subject about who is the greatest tennis player of all time. 'Roger found the whole conversation really uncomfortable. I realised at that moment that Roger wasn't at all comfortable with how great he is.'

The admiration flows both ways. Federer's worship of Sampras is no media confection. He once confessed how he felt 'starstruck' when on court with Sampras. 'When I practise with Pete, I still can't get over who he is, what he has achieved and what he means to me. I suppose I'm a little mesmerised by his game. Just being on the practice court with him is so special, and

▲ Federer blows a kiss to the Centre Court crowd.

sometimes makes it difficult to just concentrate on my shots. It always feels slightly unreal that I'm hitting balls with Pete. There's something about Pete's game, about his ball, that is so different to practising with other players. When we practise, it's always incredible.' When Federer's words were passed on, Sampras was thrilled. 'That's very flattering to hear,' he said. 'I just try to hold my own and give him a good workout.'

4
MOVES LIKE A WHISPER

JIM COURIER, A FORMER WORLD NUMBER ONE, IS NOT THE ONLY ONE WHO HALF-BELIEVES THAT WHEN FEDERER IS 'IN FULL FLIGHT', IT IS ALMOST AS IF HE IS 'FLOATING' OR 'GLIDING' ABOVE THE COURT.

R oger Federer has the quietest feet in tennis. The sound he makes as he moves about a court is just a peep or two above silence. To appreciate the lightness of Federer's movement, turn the volume up dangerously high on your television, close your eyes and listen to the hush from his side of the net. Maybe Federer's footsteps do not seem quite so remarkable on the natural surfaces of grass and clay, when others' shoes are not so noisy either. But it is on hard courts, when an opponent is stomping and squeaking along the baseline, that the contrast is clear. It is strange to think, while wondering at Federer's graceful, artistic footwork, that he is wearing shoes a size too big for him. He needs the additional room in his trainers to accommodate the second pair of socks and the tape. In others, that could result in extreme clumsiness.

Jim Courier, a former world number one, is not the only one who half-believes that when Federer is 'in full flight', it is almost as if he is 'floating' or 'gliding' above the court. Nick Bollettieri, speaking from his experience as a coach and a paratrooper, believes that Federer 'moves like a whisper', while John McEnroe has compared the Swiss to ballet dancer Mikhail Baryshnikov. Just months before becoming Federer's coach, Ivan Ljubičić observed to the *New York Times* at the 2015 Wimbledon Championships: 'Ooh, Roger's dancing again.' Footwork specialist David Bailey has identified fifteen different moves that tennis players make. If there are any other players, aside from Federer, who can perform all fifteen, there are not many of them. 'Roger's movement is difficult to teach and difficult to copy,' said Bailey, 'but, oh, so beautiful to watch.'

According to Australian Thanasi Kokkinakis, who played the role of practice partner at Federer's Dubai training camp before the 2015 season, the

▶ The way Federer moves, it is almost as if he is floating above the court.

Swiss's movement allows him to steal time. 'Roger's movement is unbelievable,' Kokkinakis said. 'He takes so much time away from you during points. There are balls that you think will just come back to you as a rally ball, and then Roger gets in behind it and takes the ball early. That makes it so tough against him. Of course, it's important for everyone to move well, but it's such a fundamental part of his game. It's such a big thing for him, taking time away from his opponent. It means that he gets you moving before you can get him moving.'

●

They say that Roger Federer does not have a sweat gland in his body. Certainly, he does not request a towel between points with anything like the frequency of some. But that is not to say he does not dab at his forehead occasionally, as a gentleman might on a warm day at Glyndebourne. Another fiction – and this is one which Rafa Nadal appears to have bought into, describing Federer as 'a blessed freak of nature' – is that the Swiss has never had to work hard at the physical side of tennis. Actually, those two myths are essentially one, this notion that Federer would never need to do anything so vulgar as exerting too much effort. It is as if Federer is seen as the last surviving amateur in an otherwise professional sport.

'I've had to push and mould my body to adapt it to cope with the repetitive muscle stress that tennis forces on you, but [Federer] just seems to have been born to play the game. His physique – his D.N.A. – seems perfectly adapted to tennis,' Nadal wrote in his autobiography. 'They tell me he doesn't train as hard as I do. I don't know if it's true, but it would figure.' It is unclear to whom Nadal has been talking about Federer's physical preparation, but it would appear he has not had a conversation with Pierre Paganini, Federer's fitness trainer. A thoughtful, shaven-headed Swiss, who first met Federer at the National Tennis Centre in Écublens, Paganini has often heard how Federer has supposedly floated his way to all those titles. 'Imagine you go to the ballet,' Paganini said. 'It looks beautiful, harmonious, graceful. It looks easy, but do we think that ballerinas don't work? Yes, they work, and they work very, very hard. It's the same with Roger, who is an artist on the court. But he has to work hard to be able to express that creativity on the court, and to be a champion. It's not possible otherwise.'

Such was Federer's talent, Paganini thought on first joining the team in 2000 that his new employer had been able to get away with not being in the best possible shape. Immediately, Paganini resolved to do something about that, though this was not a transformation that could be completed within days or even weeks; it was a process that would continue for a number of years as Federer sought a first Grand Slam singles title. Federer's victory over Pete Sampras in the fourth round of the 2001 Wimbledon Championships had shown that he had the talent to win a major, but it would not be for another couple of years before he was physically capable of putting together seven victories inside a fortnight. 'Roger is able to do a lot of things', said Paganini, 'he's very coordinated, he moves unbelievably well, and that means that he tries to do more because his game is very rich. If you have more complexity in your game, there is also more complexity to your footwork. Roger is able to do this [look as though he is gliding] as he has unbelievable potential. He feels the game very well, and if you do that you will have a creative game. From a young age you learn to move in a way that allows you to play this kind of game and to be a smart, intelligent player.'

▼ Federer is 'like an artist on the court', says his fitness trainer.

AVERAGE KILOMETRES RUN PER MATCH

Data from the 2015 Grand Slams

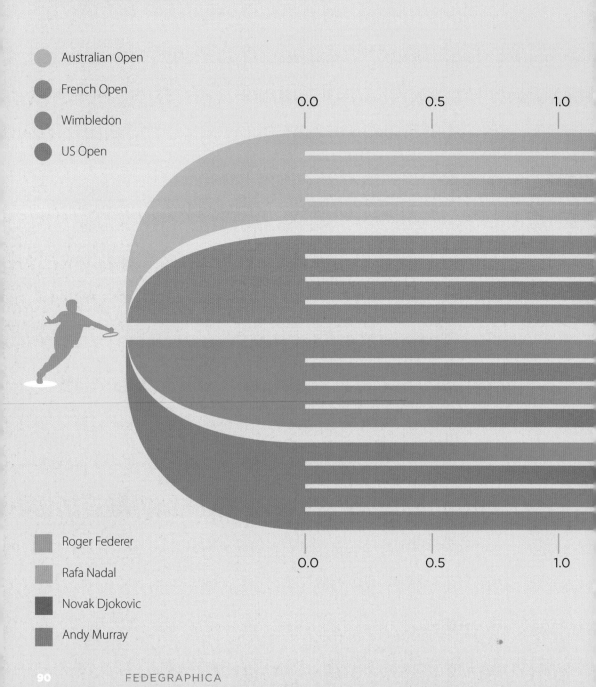

Australian Open

French Open

Wimbledon

US Open

Roger Federer

Rafa Nadal

Novak Djokovic

Andy Murray

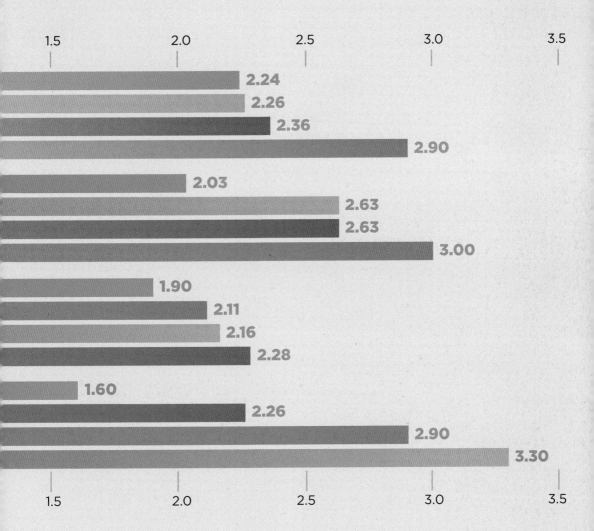

1.5 2.0 2.5 3.0 3.5

2.24
2.26
2.36
2.90

2.03
2.63
2.63
3.00

1.90
2.11
2.16
2.28

1.60
2.26
2.90
3.30

1.5 2.0 2.5 3.0 3.5

In the modern game you cannot survive on talent and artistry alone. Tennis, with its beginnings in Victorian society garden parties, has become a brutal sport. Over the course of a season Federer could find himself playing in excess of eighty matches. Sometimes, even more than ninety, such as in 2006 when he made ninety-seven singles appearances. Some of those matches could be in extreme heat. It is not unknown for players at the Australian Open to suffer ill effects, such as dizziness and blackouts, because of the weather. Even cities with mild climates, such as London, can test a player's resolve. Consider the running time for the 2009 Wimbledon final when Federer was on Centre Court for more than four hours for his victory over Andy Roddick, culminating in a 16–14 fifth set. That was around half an hour shorter than the previous summer's Wimbledon final, in which Federer lost to Nadal, though that match was broken up by rain delays. Or remember the occasion, on the very same rectangle of grass, at the 2012 Olympic tennis tournament, when Federer needed almost four and a half hours to overcome Argentina's Juan Martín del Potro in the semi-finals. And that was a three-set match, albeit the longest one in history, with a 19–17 final set.

▼ Federer's conditioning programme ensures he has explosive power, speed and endurance.

'YOU CAN PLAY FOR ONE HOUR, TWO HOURS, THREE HOURS, FOUR HOURS, AND YOU MIGHT PLAY SEVENTY OR EIGHTY MATCHES IN A YEAR. YOU'RE NOT A MARATHON RUNNER, BUT YOU NEED TO BE READY TO PLAY EIGHTY MATCHES IN A YEAR, WHICH IS A LOT. AND THE GOAL IS TO HAVE EXPLOSIVE POWER FOR THOSE EIGHTY MATCHES'.

'In tennis you need endurance and you also need explosive power and speed and acceleration,' Paganini said. 'You can play for one hour, two hours, three hours, four hours, and you might play seventy or eighty matches in a year. You're not a marathon runner, but you need to be ready to play eighty matches in a year, which is a lot. And the goal is to have explosive power for those eighty matches. The reactions and the explosive power in tennis are important because you never run a long way in tennis. You do a lot of stop and go, stop and go. You're pushing off again and again with that stop and go. And you must do it a lot of times on different surfaces, and you have to do that more or less every day, because you cannot just count the matches – you must also count the practice sessions.'

In part, the idea of Roger the Amateur has been fuelled by his decision not to invite the world to inspect his training regime. Not like others do, anyway. Novak Djokovic has written a book about how he primes his body for competition, plus how he transformed his body by cutting gluten, lactose, sugar and other vices from his diet, while adding mānuka honey and cups of liquorice tea. Andy Murray has publicised his pre-season training blocks in Miami by allowing tennis writers to puff along the sands of South Beach with him, if only for as long as is needed for photographs to be taken. Nadal makes no secret of the work that he needs to do to stay in shape. Federer, though, does not ask his agent to put all his effort on public display, though that is not to suggest he is secretive. 'People don't talk enough about how hard Roger works behind the scenes,' Tim Henman said. You need Paganini's help to peer behind the curtain, where Federer lifts weights to loud music. In the past, he has worked out to trance, other electronic music, and heavier stuff, such as Metallica and AC/DC. And he does interval training to prepare himself for the 'short bursts' of activity during a match.

It is strange to think that Federer and Nadal are the same height (1.85 metres, or six feet, one inch) and the same weight (eight-five kilograms, or thirteen stone, five pounds) when they have such different bodies. Or at least appear to. Certainly, Federer has never had biceps like Nadal's. Is Nadal right that Federer, with his lean upper body and strong legs, has the 'perfect physique' for tennis? Looking at Federer's parents, neither of whom are tall, it is

◄ Federer with
Severin Lüthi, the
Swiss Davis Cup
captain, and also
a long-standing
member of his
own entourage.

perhaps fortunate that he grew to be as tall as he is, which is close to the ideal height. We are forever being told that this is the age of the tennis giant, and that anyone short enough to be able to walk through a doorway without ducking should consider their future in the sport. But the tale of Goliaths taking over the sport has been much exaggerated. Consider the height and weight of the other elite members of tennis's golden generation. Novak Djokovic, at 1.88 metres (six feet, two inches), is fractionally taller than Federer and Nadal, while Andy Murray is the most physically imposing of the quartet at 1.91 metres (six feet, three inches), yet the four of them hardly look as though they have just stepped off a basketball court. Djokovic is the lightest of the four at seventy-eight kilograms or twelve stone, four pounds, while Murray weighs eighty-four kilograms or thirteen stone, three pounds. Clearly, if Federer were a little taller and heftier, and had longer limbs, he would probably have a little extra pop on his serve. But it is hardly as if Federer lacks for power. And there is a trade-off that comes with that extra height: if Federer were two metres tall, he might not be as good a mover, and that is such a central part of his game.

'It's difficult to answer the question of whether Roger has the ideal build for tennis,' Paganini said. 'We have to respect a great champion like Nadal, who has a very different body to Roger, who has won all those tournaments. And then you have Pete Sampras, who again has a different body to Roger's, and lots of other great champions, too. The most important thing is that you have harmony between the person you are, the player you want to be, and the physical capability you have. Of course, with Roger it's fantastic as he has that. It's just important to be yourself.'

The biggest difference between Federer and others, Tim Henman said, is that 'Roger doesn't put a lot of stress on his body'. 'You look at his physique and it's a great physique as he's very agile and has great balance. He's light on his feet, unlike other players at the top of the game, so he won't be putting as much stress on his body as someone like Nadal or Murray.'

The opening point of Federer's first-round match at the 2015 Wimbledon Championships brought up a significant statistic, and one that said much about his physical resilience and his ability to protect himself against injury. It was his sixty-third consecutive Grand Slam, a record for both sexes, putting him one ahead of Japan's Ai Sugiyama. The next men on the list behind Federer are South African Wayne Ferreira on fifty-six and his 2014-15 coach,

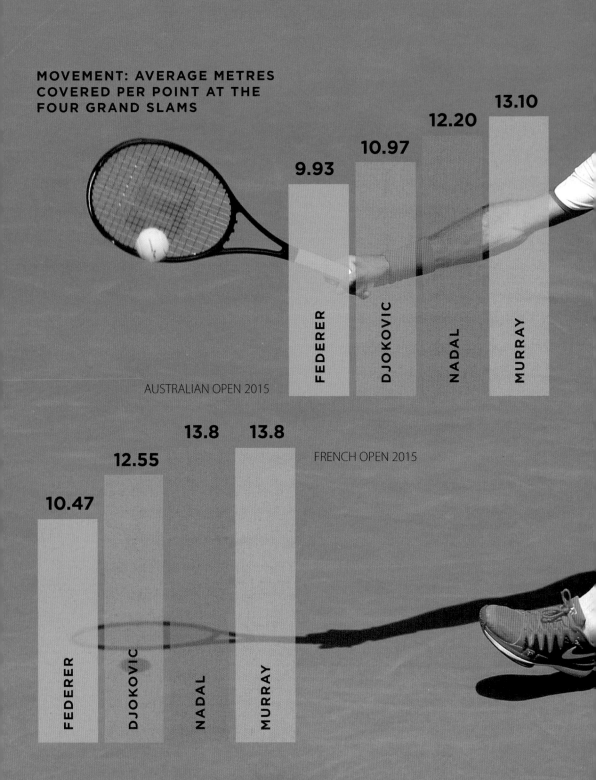

MOVEMENT: AVERAGE METRES COVERED PER POINT AT THE FOUR GRAND SLAMS

AUSTRALIAN OPEN 2015

9.93 — FEDERER
10.97 — DJOKOVIC
12.20 — NADAL
13.10 — MURRAY

FRENCH OPEN 2015

10.47 — FEDERER
12.55 — DJOKOVIC
13.8 — NADAL
13.8 — MURRAY

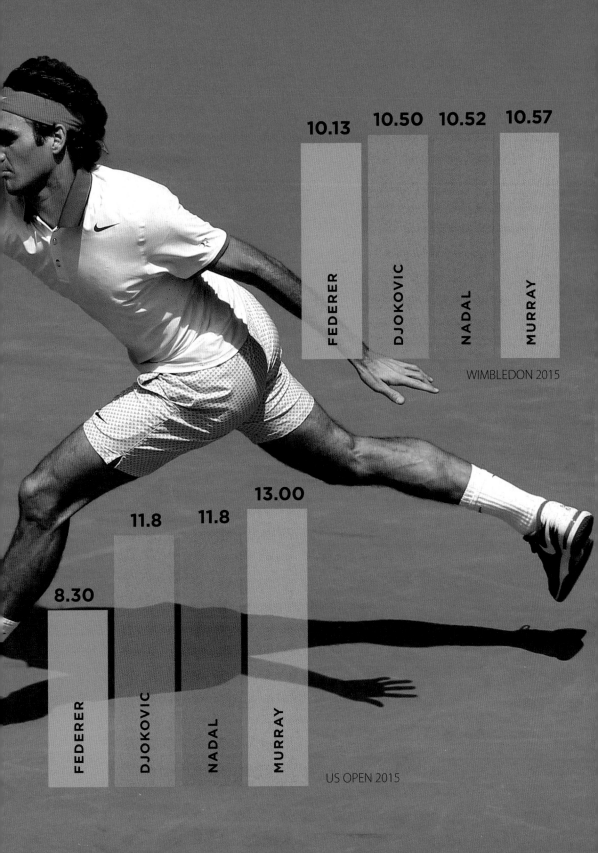

10.13 FEDERER

10.50 DJOKOVIC

10.52 NADAL

10.57 MURRAY

WIMBLEDON 2015

8.30 FEDERER

11.8 DJOKOVIC

11.8 NADAL

13.00 MURRAY

US OPEN 2015

'IMPORTANTLY, ROGER IS ABLE TO BE VERY FOCUSED WHEN IT'S IMPORTANT TO BE FOCUSED, AND HE CAN BE VERY RELAXED WHEN IT'S IMPORTANT TO BE RELAXED. HE'S VERY GOOD AT USING THE RIGHT AMOUNT OF PHYSICAL AND MENTAL ENERGY. HE WORKS IN THE RIGHT WAY AT THE RIGHT MOMENTS.'

Stefan Edberg, on fifty-four. With his appearances at the 2015 US Open and 2016 Australian Open, Federer extended that figure to sixty-five consecutive majors.

At the time of writing, Federer has never retired from a match he has started – another remarkable statistic – and has only ever withdrawn in the middle of an event three times. The third such occasion was the final of the 2014 season-ending tournament in London, when a back injury prevented him from playing Djokovic. How Nadal would have loved to have been as free of injury as Federer has been. 'The rest of us just have to learn to live with pain, and long breaks from the game, because a foot, a shoulder, or a leg has sent a cry for help to the brain asking it to stop,' the Majorcan has observed. Nadal's knees have been the prime reason for his long absences from the sport, while Murray has missed Grand Slams because of wrist and back problems. When he was still full of gluten, Djokovic, too, had physical issues. In his youth, he was notorious for not liking hot days, and had difficulties with his breathing. More reason, then, for those three to talk more about their physical regimes now, perhaps to bolster their psyches.

It is true that good fortune has played a part in Federer avoiding serious injury for so long. But this is not just about luck. Paganini spoke of Federer's ability to use the right amount of energy – he can distinguish between working hard and over-training, and will not flog himself to exhaustion. 'Importantly, Roger is able to be very focused when it's important to be focused, and he can be very relaxed when it's important to be relaxed. He's very good at using the right amount of physical and mental energy. He works in the right way at the right moments,' Paganini said. 'To work hard is one thing. It's another thing to know when to work hard and when to rest, and for how long. It's when you work on the right things at the right time, and with the right amount of energy, that you get the greatest benefit.'

No detail is too small to be ignored. 'In sport, as in life, you look at the details and then when you put all those details together, it amounts to a lot,' Paganini said. That attention to detail extends to Federer's sleep and diet. Ideally, Federer has ten hours of sleep a night. Anything less than that and there is a danger of Federer waking up and thinking, 'Ugh, I'm exhausted'. Federer tends to eat porridge and berries on the morning of a match. He

▲ Federer tends
to eat porridge
and berries on
the morning of a
match.

would prefer to have a plate of croissants. In fact, Federer is not much of a breakfast person. He prefers lunch and dinner, but again he is aware of the need to be professional. As a young man Federer was fussy, as well as a vegetarian. His former coach Peter Lundgren remembers how in Federer's youth there were only two dishes the player would order in restaurants: gnocchi with gorgonzola and pasta with tomato sauce. The turning point came the night Federer went to dinner with Switzerland's Davis Cup squad and ordered rice in a steakhouse. Marc Rosset, one of the senior players, asked the waitress for a selection of eight different meats and had Federer try them all. It was an experience which turned him back into a carnivore. These days Federer is much more of a culinary adventurer. But, as is the case with most tennis players, his diet is heavy on pasta. 'Because of the travelling you always

LONGEST MATCHES

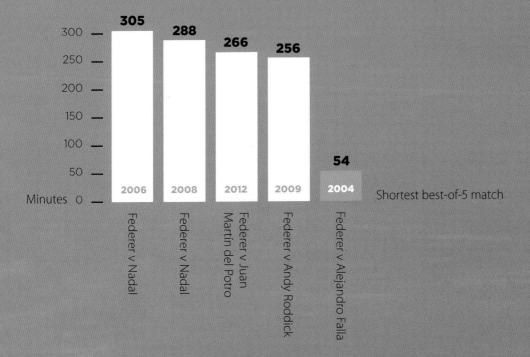

305	**288**	**266**	**256**	**54**	Shortest best-of-5 match
2006	2008	2012	2009	2004	
Federer v Nadal	Federer v Nadal	Federer v Juan Martín del Potro	Federer v Andy Roddick	Federer v Alejandro Falla	

Minutes: 0, 50, 100, 150, 200, 250, 300

05:05 Federer lost a five-setter to Rafa Nadal in the 2006 Rome final.

04:48 Federer's five-set defeat to Rafa Nadal in the 2008 Wimbledon final, interrupted by rain breaks, took 4 hours and 48 minutes, which made it the longest Wimbledon final of all time.

04:26 Federer's victory over Juan Martín del Potro in the semi-finals of the 2012 Olympic tournament at the All England Club had a running time of 4 hours and 26 minutes – it was the longest best-of-three-sets match since tennis turned professional in 1968.

04:16 Federer's victory over Andy Roddick in the 2009 Wimbledon final, which culminated with a 16–14 fifth set, lasted for 77 games, which was a record for a Wimbledon final.

00:54 Federer's shortest best-of-five-set match came against Colombia's Alejandro Falla in the second round of the 2004 Wimbledon Championships, which he won in 54 minutes.

want to grab the safe bet. And the safe bet is always pasta.'

Tennis players fear a diagnosis of glandular fever, or mononucleosis, and rightly so as it can end careers. While the disease did not bring Federer's tennis career to a close, it did have a considerable effect on his fitness levels during 2008. That was the year he lost in the semi-finals of the Australian Open to Djokovic, won just four games in the French Open final against Nadal, and when his five years of Wimbledon domination came to an end with defeat in the final against the Spaniard. Federer has estimated that he lost as many as twenty training days to the disease, though he was unaware for a long time that he even had it. Had his doctors known at the time, they would have advised strongly against playing the Australian Open.

Federer has not escaped without physical ailments. That would have been an impossibility. It is a near-certainty for any tennis player that they will have to deal with some illness and injury, and that is true even if they pay as much attention to their body and physical conditioning as Federer does. In 2013, Federer did suffer with a bad back, with his results so mixed that some observers made the error of suggesting retirement. His back problems flared up again in late 2014, which was why he withdrew from the final of the season-ending tournament. 'You cannot play more than a thousand matches and go without injuries,' Paganini said. But it was only in early 2016 that Federer had an operation for the first time, which was needed after damaging his knee running a bath for his children (as opposed to, say, running down a forehand out wide). And that's quite something: how many other players can reach their mid-thirties without previously going under the surgeon's knife? As a result of the injury Federer didn't play at the 2016 French Open, the first Grand Slam he had missed this century.

▶ In his mid-thirties, Federer is in great physical condition.

FEDERER V MURRAY

Movement heat map, London Olympics Gold Medal Match, 2012

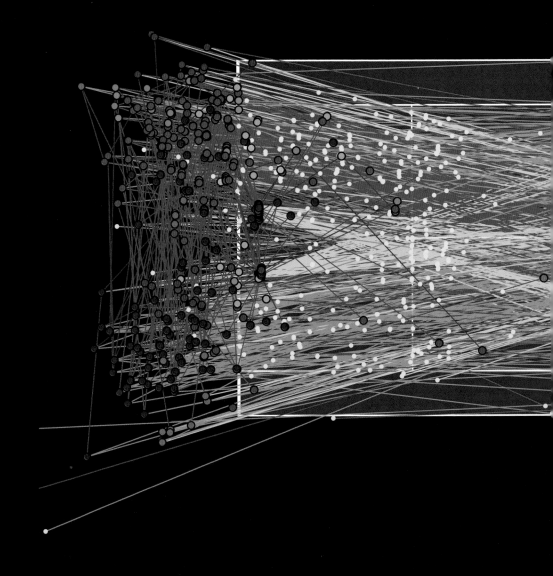

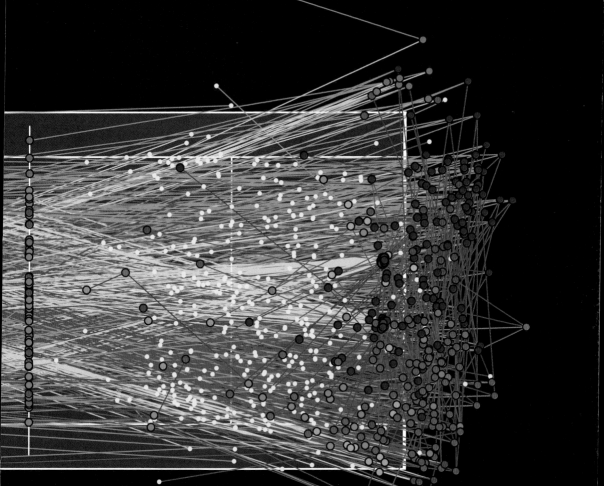

5
STRUNG TIGHT

FOR EACH MATCH AT A GRAND SLAM, FEDERER WILL
TAKE EIGHT OR NINE RACKETS ON COURT, STRUNG AT THE
TENSIONS HE HAS CHOSEN, RISING FOR GREATER CONTROL
AND DIPPING FOR MORE POWER. HALF A KILOGRAM HERE OR
THERE COULD BE THE DIFFERENCE BETWEEN VICTORY AND
DEFEAT.

Late every evening during tournaments, usually after he has returned from dinner, Roger Federer composes a text message. Contained in the message, which he will ping to his racket-stringer, are two or three numbers: the tensions he has selected for his match the next day. Those tensions, expressed in kilograms, will determine Federer's ability to play the tennis he wants. Let those numbers also stand as examples of the detail that goes into Federer's preparation. For each match at a Grand Slam, Federer will take eight or nine rackets on court, strung at the tensions he has chosen, rising for greater control and dipping for more power. Much thought goes into that message. Half a kilogram here or there could be the difference between victory and defeat. 'The question that Roger will be asking himself before he sends that text message is, "How are the balls flying?"' said Nate Ferguson, whose company, P1 or Priority 1, has been looking after Federer's rackets for more than a decade.

'Whether the balls are flying or not depends on the surface, the altitude and also the ball manufacturer. Sometimes they fluff up quickly and those become slow balls, dead balls. Then we look at the match conditions – the opponent and the weather. The higher the temperature, the more the ball flies. The higher the altitude, and the thinner the air, the more the ball flies. All these factors combined make it a heavy ball, a normal ball, or a fast ball. Based on that, he will decide on the tensions he wants,' said Ferguson.

The two have bonded over the years and it is not difficult to understand why a friendship might develop between Federer and the man who oversees the stringing of his rackets. Without his 'bats' Federer would be nowhere, a point reinforced every time he steps on to an aeroplane, which is a great deal.

▶ Federer pays
close attention to
the small details.

PERCENTAGE OF RETURN GAMES WON

(correct up to end of 2017 season)

Modern players

27 Federer

32 Murray

32 Djokovic

33 Nadal

Former champions

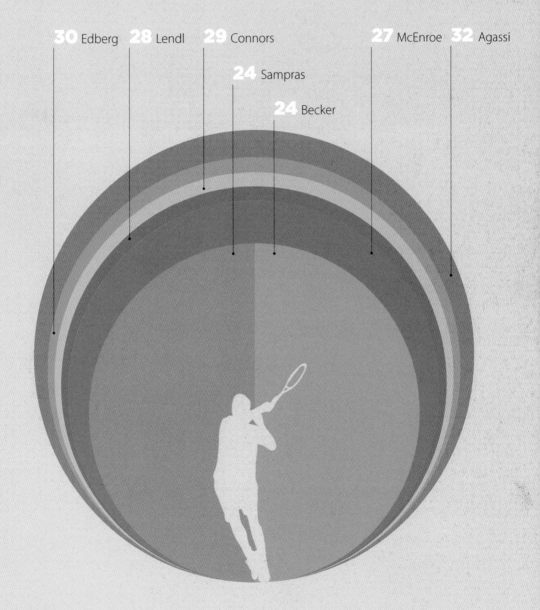

30 Edberg   **28** Lendl   **29** Connors   **27** McEnroe   **32** Agassi

24 Sampras

24 Becker

THE JOB OF LOOKING
AFTER FEDERER'S
RACKETS COMES WITH
GREAT RESPONSIBILITY,
AND JUST FLEETING
GLAMOUR. FERGUSON
RECALLED THE NIGHT
HE ANSWERED THE
DOOR OF THE HOUSE
HE HAD RENTED IN
WIMBLEDON VILLAGE
TO FIND FEDERER
STANDING THERE IN A
DINNER JACKET.

One of the advantages of flying privately is that he can take the frames into the cabin with him. Travelling first-class on commercial flights, Federer is often able to carry the rackets as hand-luggage, but there is no guarantee of that as some airlines class them as potential weapons. 'If Roger has to check his rackets in the hold, that's going to make for a nervous flight,' said Ferguson.

The job of looking after Federer's rackets comes with great responsibility, and just fleeting glamour. Ferguson recalled the night he answered the door of the house he had rented in Wimbledon Village to find Federer standing there in a dinner jacket. It was the Sunday evening at the conclusion of the 2004 Wimbledon Championships, and Federer, having retained his title that afternoon, was on his way to the Champions' Dinner. For a racket-stringer, used to being backstage, this was close to being a cinematic moment. Federer had come to confirm he wanted Ferguson to take care of his rackets on a permanent basis. He had been on a trial since the clay-court tournament in Hamburg that spring. 'Let's do this,' said the man in the tuxedo, and Ferguson and his team of stringers have been around ever since. Federer pays Priority 1 an annual retainer of around $40,000 to care for his rackets at the Grand Slams and the Masters-level tournaments.

For another example of the patterns and order that help to shape Federer's existence – above his serving patterns and the way he deploys his forehand – consider how he switches his racket at every ball-change. That is, after the opening seven games of a match, and from then on after every nine games. However, it is not quite as simple as that. The exact timing of the swap depends on whether Federer is about to serve, in which case the switch will come a game before or a game after the ball-change. He does not want to be adjusting to both new balls and new strings at the same time. On top of everything else that is happening in a match, Ferguson said, Federer is 'keeping track of those numbers when no one else is'. There is a little theatre in the moment Federer unsheathes the racket from the plastic bag stamped with the R.F. logo. Each of the bags has a sticker attached so Federer can find the racket he wants easily. Applying those logos and stickers is just one small part of the process in preparing Federer's rackets, with each one taking around half an hour.

CONVERTING AND SAVING BREAK POINTS

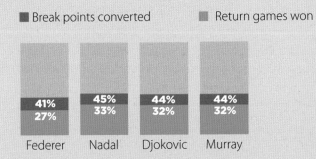

■ Break points converted   ■ Return games won

41%	**45%**	**44%**	**44%**
27%	**33%**	**32%**	**32%**
Federer	Nadal	Djokovic	Murray

CAREER BREAK POINT CONVERSION RATE

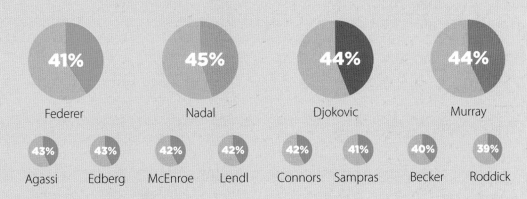

41%	45%	44%	44%
Federer	Nadal	Djokovic	Murray

43%	43%	42%	42%	42%	41%	40%	39%
Agassi	Edberg	McEnroe	Lendl	Connors	Sampras	Becker	Roddick

CAREER BREAK POINTS SAVED

67%	66%	65%	63%
Federer	Nadal	Djokovic	Murray

68%	68%	66%	65%	64%	63%	62%	58%
Sampras	Roddick	Becker	Agassi	Edberg	Lendl	McEnroe	Connors

▲ Federer
celebrates
winning his first
Wimbledon title
with his then
coach Peter
Lundgren.

For about as long as Ferguson has strung rackets for him, Federer has played with natural gut in his sixteen main strings and polyester on the nineteen cross strings. 'It's a great combination. He can swing out because the deadness of the polyester means you can hit the ball harder and still have control. The ball suddenly dives into court because of the topspin that Roger is applying to the ball. But if he went all polyester – so in the main and cross strings – it would take the level of control up higher, but it would be harder on his arm and his wrist and it would be more difficult to generate pace. So Roger uses half and half as then he has a mix of that good, resilient string, which gives you good feel, with the dead, controllable polyester,' Ferguson said. 'And, importantly, the strings stick together and don't move around so much. Remember how Pete Sampras, who played only with natural gut, would be clicking his strings after every point to straighten them out, so he didn't have the big gaps that would have given him uncontrollable power? This combination of gut and polyester stays much straighter, which enhances the ability to control the spin of the ball.'

Ferguson does not personally attend to all of Federer's rackets. But Federer could not have anyone better qualified to oversee their care. For years Ferguson travelled with Sampras as his personal stringer, and no one in the history of tennis has been as obsessive about his rackets as Sampras was. 'He would want them strung very tightly with super-thin, very fragile gut strings. He was also very pernickety about the handle,' Ferguson recalled. While Federer could never match those Sampras levels of fussiness, the Swiss has his own quirks. In addition to re-gripping the racket, and applying a red Wilson stencil to the strings, Priority 1 are asked to add plastic 'string savers', even though Ferguson said they bring no real benefit. 'For a guy like Roger who is getting all those rackets restrung for every match, is this really going to help? But here's the thing – I don't bring this up with Roger, and no one else in the company brings it up either. When he came to us, he was number one in the world and he had those string savers in. So we're not going to mess with that. Those string savers can be hard to come by, but we make sure we find them and put them in every racket we string for him.'

Despite their friendship, there is one thing that Federer will not do for Ferguson: give him the broken racket that he wants for his collection of twisted frames. At home in Florida, Ferguson has a display in his workshop of some of his clients' busted rackets. There is a lot of anger, frustration, nihilism and history in those splintered, crumpled frames. 'It's a collection of the rackets that clients have smashed at important times, which I started with one of Pete's,' he said. For rarity value, nothing tops a racket broken by Federer. While Federer has given Ferguson one of the rackets he used to win the 2009 French Open, which completed his career Grand Slam, that is not the one Ferguson covets. The one he would like is the racket that Federer destroyed during a semi-final defeat by Novak Djokovic at the hard-court tournament in Miami in 2009. That was the mildly shocking occasion when Federer reacted to duffing a midcourt forehand by giving his frame a full-blooded whack on to the ground, and then tossing the broken frame across the court. 'That's the racket I really want,' Ferguson said. 'I would like any racket he smashes on court during a match, but, of course, he doesn't do that anymore.'

●

It is the porter service that makes your nerves fizz like a dropped bottle of cola. 'Empty and awkward,' Roger Federer has said of walking on to Centre Court without a bag, a racket or any other prop in hand. For the first six rounds of the Wimbledon fortnight players carry their own bags out on to the lawn.

WINNERS AND UNFORCED ERRORS

The average number of winners and unforced errors per set in the Grand Slam finals Federer won.

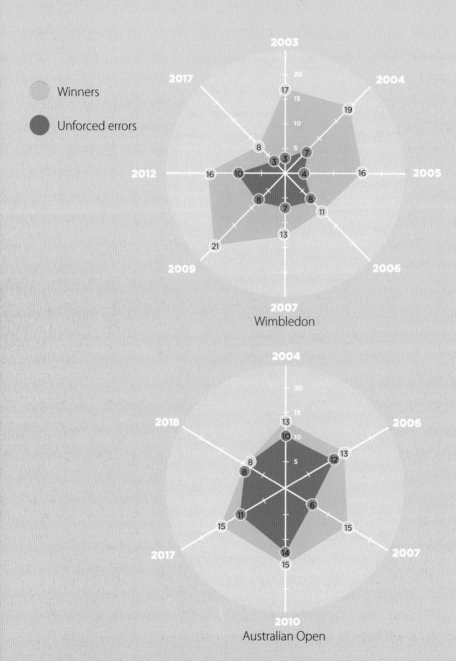

Winners

Unforced errors

Wimbledon

Australian Open

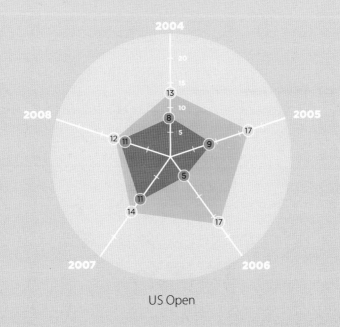

US Open

Average number of winners and unforced errors per set in the Grand Slam finals Federer won.

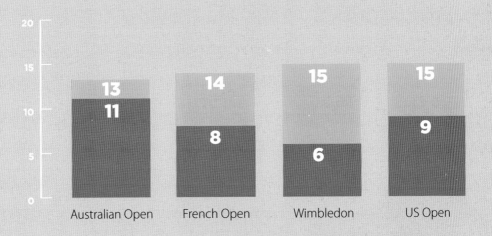

The choreography changes for the final when the locker-room attendants accompany the competitors on to the grass. This break from the norm can make players feel out of sorts, even downright uncomfortable, only adding, in some cases, to the sense of bewilderment. In 2003, his first Wimbledon final, this porter service was new to Federer, and also to his Australian opponent, Mark Philippoussis.

Pause the Federer story at that moment, at that first frame as the players and the attendants come into view. As the tennis Sherpas bring the rackets and other kit out into the stadium that day, with a new Wimbledon champion guaranteed, who could have imagined that one of the players would go on to eclipse Pete Sampras, who just the season before had won his fourteenth major at the 2002 US Open, while the other would never play in another Grand Slam final? Now fast-forward to the summer of 2015, when one of the protagonists would appear in his tenth Wimbledon final, while the other would take a wild card into the qualifying competition for a tournament in Newport, Rhode Island. That, incidentally, turned out to be a comeback that went nowhere fast as Philippoussis was beaten in the first round of the

AGE WHEN WINNING FIRST GRAND SLAM
A selection of ATP players

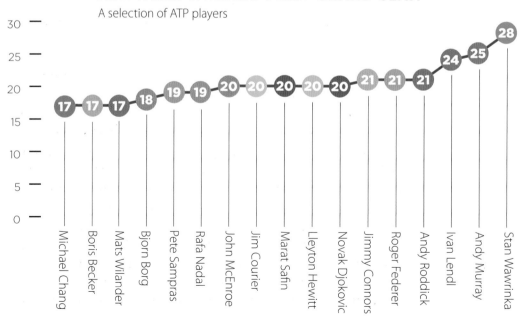

'I DON'T KNOW HOW LONG I'LL NEED TO GET OVER THIS DEFEAT,' FEDERER SAID IN HIS POST-MATCH DEBRIEF. 'A DAY, A WEEK, A YEAR – OR MY ENTIRE CAREER.' IN THEIR HEADLINE THE NEXT MORNING THE FRENCH NEWSPAPER *L'ÉQUIPE* DESCRIBED FEDERER AS BEING 'SHIPWRECKED IN QUIET WATERS'.

preliminaries. However, on that Sunday afternoon in London back in 2003, no one foresaw quite such a divergence in fortunes for the pair. To Philippoussis's mind the Wimbledon title was there for the taking. 'It had always been a dream of mine to play in a Wimbledon final – it was the tournament I had watched as a little kid – and it was special walking out to play against Roger that day. I felt good as I walked out on to Centre Court. I was confident I would win,' Philippoussis remembered, more than a decade later.

After all, Philippoussis had only recently defeated Federer at a tournament in Hamburg on a clay court, a surface supposed to favour Federer. So, surely, grass would help someone with a serve so powerful, if occasionally a little wayward, that he had been given the nickname 'Scud'? And while Federer had no previous experience of the extra pressures of playing in a Grand Slam final, Philippoussis had been runner-up to Pat Rafter at the 1998 US Open. Until that Wimbledon fortnight Federer had never gone beyond the quarter-finals of a Grand Slam. For all the promise that Federer had demonstrated at Wimbledon in 2001, when he defeated Sampras in the fourth round, concerns had developed since about his ability to deal with the mental aspect of challenging for the sport's biggest prizes. Federer's talent was not in doubt. But could he cope with the expectation?

When Federer failed to win a round at either of the European Slams in 2002 he suffered a crisis of confidence. He felt dragged down mentally. His coach, Peter Lundgren, thought the player was no longer himself on the court. There was worse to come at the 2003 French Open, just a month before the start of Wimbledon, with a first-round defeat by Peruvian Luis Horna that was profoundly troubling for those who believed in Federer's talent. 'I don't know how long I'll need to get over this defeat,' Federer said in his post-match debrief. 'A day, a week, a year – or my entire career.' In their headline the next morning the French newspaper *L'Équipe* described Federer as being 'Shipwrecked in Quiet Waters'. Since beating Sampras in 2001 at Wimbledon, Federer had failed to win another Grand Slam match in Europe. In years to come, when Federer looked back at defeats like those, what upset him was not so much that he had lost, but that he had that 'terrible feeling of leaving

WINNING PERCENTAGE AFTER LOSING THE FIRST SET

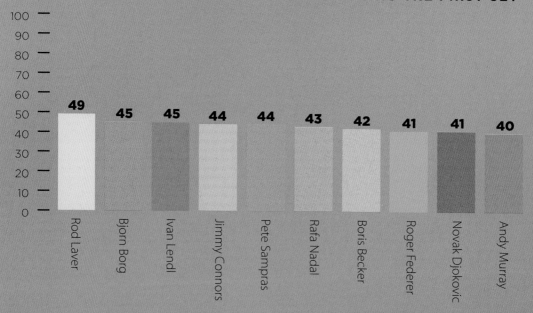

	49	45	45	44	44	43	42	41	41	40
	Rod Laver	Bjorn Borg	Ivan Lendl	Jimmy Connors	Pete Sampras	Rafa Nadal	Boris Becker	Roger Federer	Novak Djokovic	Andy Murray

WINNING PERCENTAGE AFTER TAKING THE FIRST SET

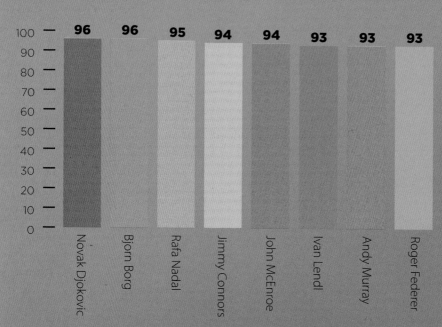

	96	96	95	94	94	93	93	93
	Novak Djokovic	Bjorn Borg	Rafa Nadal	Jimmy Connors	John McEnroe	Ivan Lendl	Andy Murray	Roger Federer

WINNING PERCENTAGE IN FIFTH SET

	Rafa Nadal	Novak Djokovic	Andy Murray	Roger Federer
100				
90				
80	77	76		
70			71	
60				55
50				
40				
30				
20				
10				
0				

All data correct up to end of 2015 season

LITTLE DID THEY KNOW THAT THE AGE OF FEDERER, A GOLDEN TIME FOR TENNIS AESTHETES, WAS ABOUT TO BEGIN.

the court knowing I had more in me'.

The day Federer played in his first Grand Slam final he was a few weeks away from turning twenty-two. Not old by any means, but older than when many other serial Grand Slam champions captured their first majors. Rafa Nadal was nineteen when he won his first (the 2005 French Open) and Novak Djokovic was twenty (the 2008 Australian Open). 'People had been expecting Roger to do so much better,' Lundgren said, 'but mentally he wasn't ready, and he wasn't mature enough.' At that stage it was not yet apparent to Lundgren how much of an impact Peter Carter's death had had on Federer. Federer's body had also been a concern earlier in the Championships: he had been in pain after injuring his back while hitting a serve in the warm-up for the fourth-round match against Spain's Feliciano López. He could barely sit down, never mind serve or return, and he gave serious consideration to retiring from the tournament. What would be the point in continuing? However, the painkillers kicked in quickly enough to keep him in the draw.

It is tempting to think that there was some kind of historical inevitability that Federer would defeat Philippoussis to win the first of a record number of Grand Slam titles. But that is certainly not how it appeared at the time. 'You can enthral all you want about Federer's talent and potential,' John McEnroe wrote in a newspaper column on the morning of the final, 'but first he has to confirm it out there on a centre court before millions of viewers by winning a major. And the outcome of his final against Philippoussis is far from being a foregone conclusion …' No one had foreseen how the most artistic of tennis players was about to start dominating the sport. Why, only a couple of days before the final, McEnroe, Boris Becker and Martina Navratilova had been among the signatories of an open letter to the president of the International Tennis Federation, Francesco Ricci Bitti. In it they called much of modern tennis 'unbalanced and one-dimensional', and suggested that racket-heads should be reduced in size. Little did they know that the Age of Federer, a golden time for tennis aesthetes, was about to begin.

Even now, it still pains Philippoussis to think about the forehand volley he missed in the first-set tiebreak, when he already led by a mini-break. The ball landed just a few millimetres out. Philippoussis's mini-break was lost, and Federer took the breaker and the momentum, winning the match in straight sets. At the Old Boys Tennis Club, Seppli Kacovsky said they cried and drank

Champagne. There were also tears from Federer. 'Beating me that day was just the start of it for Roger,' Philippoussis said. 'He then went on that incredible run, dominating tennis as no one has ever done before. Did I think at the time he was capable of winning several Grand Slams and becoming the world number one? Absolutely. Did I think he would go on to dominate tennis like he did? No. Would Roger himself have imagined he would go on to dominate like that? No, I don't think so. What he went on to do was so special. He's so incredibly talented and as he got more and more confident he would reach a point where he felt that, no matter what he did, he wasn't going to lose. But thinking about what Roger went on to do in tennis, that doesn't make that defeat any easier to take.'

'The future has come today,' Federer's idol, Boris Becker, remarked from his position in the BBC commentary box on Centre Court. The German went on to describe the new Wimbledon champion as 'the complete package, poetry in motion'.

That evening, Federer would be in his tuxedo at the Savoy Hotel on the Strand in central London, eating a five-course champions' dinner: smoked salmon parcel with avocado mousse; tomato-infused chicken consommé; tournedos of beef with wild mushrooms; chocolate mille-feuille; coffee and petits fours. All washed down with wine, port and cognac. During his speech Federer told his fellow members of the All England Club – he had become a member by winning the tournament – that 'it would give me pleasure to hit a few balls around at leisure, and whoever would like to play me should simply give me a call'. Two days later he would land by private jet in Gstaad, the so-called Wimbledon of the Alps, where the tournament director would honour Switzerland's first male Grand Slam singles champion by presenting him with a cow called Juliette, wearing flowers and a traditional bell. The farmer's excitable voice bounced around the stadium as he declared: 'This cow weighs 800 kilos but has half the power of one of Roger's serves.'

Tennis' dirty little secret, Andre Agassi once observed, is that winning your first Grand Slam title changes nothing, apart from gaining all the trappings of success (dinner, jet, cow). That might have been true of Agassi, whose first major also came at Wimbledon, in 1992. But that certainly was not the case with Federer, who likened his affectionate

'WHAT HE WENT ON TO DO WAS SO SPECIAL. HE'S SO INCREDIBLY TALENTED AND AS HE GOT MORE AND MORE CONFIDENT HE WOULD REACH A POINT WHERE HE FELT THAT, NO MATTER WHAT HE DID, HE WASN'T GOING TO LOSE.'

FEDERER GRAND SLAM TIMELINE

	2003	2004	2005	2006	2007	2008	2009	2010
AUSTRALIAN OPEN	4TH ROUND	CHAMPION	SEMI-FINAL	CHAMPION	CHAMPION	SEMI-FINAL	FINAL	CHAMPION
FRENCH OPEN	1ST ROUND	3RD ROUND	SEMI-FINAL	FINAL	FINAL	FINAL	CHAMPION **4**	QUARTER FINAL
WIMBLEDON	CHAMPION **1**	CHAMPION	CHAMPION	CHAMPION	CHAMPION **2**	FINAL	CHAMPION **5**	QUARTER FINAL
US OPEN	4TH ROUND	CHAMPION	CHAMPION	CHAMPION	CHAMPION	CHAMPION **3**	FINAL	SEMI-FINAL

1
'THE FUTURE HAS COME TODAY.'
BORIS BECKER AFTER WATCHING ROGER FEDERER WINNING HIS FIRST GRAND SLAM TITLE AT THE 2003 WIMBLEDON CHAMPIONSHIPS.

2
FEDERER BECAME ONLY THE SECOND MAN, AFTER BJORN BORG, TO WIN FIVE SUCCESSIVE WIMBLEDON TITLES.

3
FEDERER BECAME THE FIRST MAN IN THE OPEN ERA TO WIN FIVE SUCCESSIVE US OPEN TITLES.

2011	2012	2013	2014	2015	2016	2017	2018
SEMI-FINAL	SEMI-FINAL	SEMI-FINAL	SEMI-FINAL	3RD ROUND	SEMI-FINAL	CHAMPION **6**	CHAMPION
FINAL	SEMI-FINAL	QUARTER FINAL	4TH ROUND	QUARTER FINAL	DID NOT PLAY	DID NOT PLAY	
QUARTER FINAL	CHAMPION	2ND ROUND	FINAL	FINAL	SEMI-FINAL	CHAMPION **7**	
SEMI-FINAL	QUARTER FINAL	4TH ROUND	SEMI-FINAL	FINAL	DID NOT PLAY	QUARTER FINAL	

4
FEDERER WAS 27 YEARS OLD WHEN HE COMPLETED THE CAREER GRAND SLAM (WINNING ALL FOUR MAJORS AT LEAST ONCE) WITH HIS VICTORY AT THE 2009 FRENCH OPEN.

5
BY WINNING HIS 15TH GRAND SLAM, FEDERER BECAME THE MOST SUCCESSFUL MAN IN TENNIS HISTORY, MOVING PAST PETE SAMPRAS' MARK OF 14 MAJORS.

6
RETURNING FROM A SIX-MONTH ABSENCE, FEDERER TOOK HIS FIRST GRAND SLAM TITLE FOR FIVE YEARS.

7
FEDERER BECAME THE FIRST MAN TO WIN EIGHT WIMBLEDON TITLES. HE WAS ALSO, AT THE AGE OF 35, THE OLDEST WIMBLEDON CHAMPION IN HISTORY.

WINNING CHANGED
ALMOST EVERYTHING,
INCLUDING HOW HE FELT
ABOUT HIMSELF, HIS
STANDING AMONG HIS
PEERS, AND HIS FUTURE
AMBITIONS.

embrace of Wimbledon's Challenge Cup to cuddling a new-born baby. Winning changed almost everything, including how he felt about himself, his standing among his peers, and his future ambitions.

A new Federer emerged, and there was a hardness to this relaunched model. There is no better example of that than the backstage episode at the 2003 season-ending championships in Texas at Houston's West Side Club. Just before Federer was due on court the tournament chairman, Jim McIngvale, a bedding tycoon known locally as 'Mattress Mack', sought out the Swiss in his dressing room to rebuke him for comments he had made about the quality of the facilities. These included, allegedly, a wonky court and, on one occasion, having to practise without a net. Though initially unsettled by the conversation, Federer gathered himself and staved off Andre Agassi's match point for a round-robin victory. In fact, Federer would defeat Agassi twice in a week in front of a wildly pro-Agassi crowd, the second time in the final, much to the tycoon's displeasure.

Then, just days later, this new galvanised Federer ended his collaboration with Lundgren, an association that went back to the days at Biel when the Swiss had been a teenager with plenty of promise but without a senior world ranking. From those beginnings the partnership would go on to score a Wimbledon title. No wonder this decision had required 'a lot of hard thinking' on Federer's part. Their dynamic had changed with that victory at the All England Club, Federer believed. 'You're looking up to your coach before, and all of a sudden the coach is looking up at you.' Some of the respect Federer had once had for Lundgren had seeped away. Within a couple of days of going on holiday, a seemingly restless Federer called his fitness trainer to press him for details of the programme he was planning. 'Roger, you have to wake up because the train is leaving,' Federer thought to himself. 'And you have to be on that train.'

The biggest transformation in Federer? How he now believed in himself. A first Slam had removed the self-doubt. Federer had always thought he had what it took in his racket hand to win majors. But the question he had kept on asking himself was: 'Do I have it in my mind and my legs?' Now he had answered his own query. McEnroe had imagined that winning a first Wimbledon title would give Federer a 'psychological lift'. More like a psychological lift-off.

▶ The joy of winning Wimbledon.

6
THE
GREATEST

'HE'S ALWAYS CHANGING IT UP, AND THE REASON HE DOES THAT IS THAT HE'S ABLE TO. I THINK HE HAS THE MOST CAPABILITIES AND DIMENSIONS OF ANY TENNIS PLAYER I'VE EVER KNOWN.'

———

How you view Roger Federer's game depends on your position in the stadium. The galleries see the elegance in Federer's game. Federer is thinking, among other things, about the structure, the patterns. The opponent, though, sees only chaos and disorder. A couple of players have been given the nickname 'Baby Federer'. First it was Richard Gasquet, then Grigor Dimitrov. It flattered them. There is no one who plays tennis like Federer. Not even close. 'Roger is able to do so many different things that every single time you play him, even though you might go into the match with a plan to play in a certain way, he might have a goal to do something completely different. And then you're the one adjusting,' Canadian Milos Raonic said. 'He can play one match against you chipping every single return, and then he'll play you the next time, and even though he beat you the previous time by chipping, now he's going over the ball. He's always changing it up, and the reason he does that is that he's able to. I think he has the most capabilities and dimensions of any tennis player I've ever known.'

Like everyone else in tennis, Federer's boyhood idols struggle to think of how they might unsettle and challenge Federer. Pete Sampras, for one, observed that there are 'no holes in Roger's game', not when he has 'imagination, touch, feel, a sense of the court, and [a clear vision of] how he wants to play'. On returning to elite tennis in 2014 as Novak Djokovic's coach, Boris Becker often found himself considering how the Serbian should approach matches with Federer. But he admitted: 'You will have a hard time trying to find a strategy of how to play Roger because he doesn't have a weakness.' There are no limits, Becker says, to what Federer can do with a tennis ball: 'You can't really describe Roger as a baseliner and you can't

▶ Some of Federer's best performances have come at the US Open.

describe him as a serve-and-volleyer. He can do anything.' But it was one of Federer's opponents in a Grand Slam final, Andre Agassi, who said it best, in the moments after losing to Federer at the conclusion of the 2005 US Open. 'There's only so long you can go on denying it: he's the best player I've played against. Sampras was great, no question, but there was a place to get to with Pete. You knew what you had to do. If you did it, it could be on your terms. There's no such place like that with Roger. There's a sense of urgency on every point, on every shot. If you do what you're supposed to do, you feel like it gives you a chance to win the point. That's just too good. He plays the game in a special way that I haven't seen before.'

●

Roger Federer and his future wife, Mirka Vavrinec, were lying on a beach. It was the start of the off-season, at the conclusion of the 2004 tennis year, and Federer was so mentally and physically depleted that he barely had the energy to haul himself up from the sun-lounger to order some drinks. They lay there in silence for a while. And then Mirka – this had clearly been on her mind during the silence – turned to Federer and said: 'Jesus, Roger, I can't believe what you've been doing, winning all those matches and all those tournaments.' For a number of years this became almost a ritual: Mirka would make her post-season remarks from a sun-lounger and they would make Federer about as happy as he would be all year. As Federer would say after one of those debriefs: 'I don't often get the chance to reflect on what I have achieved, and it usually happens when I'm on vacation and I'm talking to Mirka. That's always a great moment for me when Mirka tells me she is proud of me for handling everything. Those are the times when I feel really good about myself.'

AFTER BEATING MARAT SAFIN IN THE FINAL, FEDERER RECEIVED THIS COMPLIMENT FROM THE RUSSIAN: 'I'VE JUST LOST TO A MAGICIAN.' AND THEN THIS FROM THE WATCHING JOHN McENROE: 'ROGER MIGHT JUST BE THE SMOOTHEST, MOST TALENTED PLAYER I'VE EVER SET EYES ON.'

Federer's talent burned through the opposition and the history books. Toni Nadal says that from 2004 to 2007 Federer was not just the finest tennis player, but also nothing short of being 'the greatest athlete in the world'. During those golden years Federer was essentially unbeatable on almost every court on the tennis map. It was only when playing Rafa Nadal at Roland Garros, or other stops of the European clay-court circuit, that Federer

SEEKING PERFECTION –
WHAT YEAR WAS FEDERER AT HIS MOST DOMINANT?

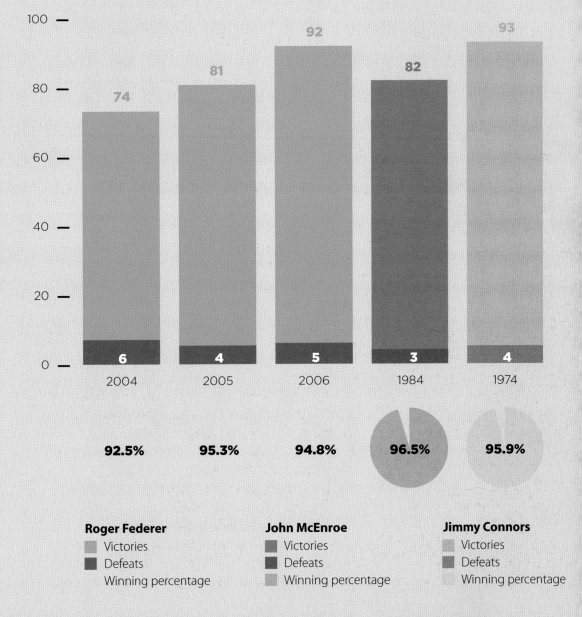

74	81	92	82	93
6	4	5	3	4
2004	2005	2006	1984	1974
92.5%	95.3%	94.8%	96.5%	95.9%

Roger Federer
- Victories
- Defeats
- Winning percentage

John McEnroe
- Victories
- Defeats
- Winning percentage

Jimmy Connors
- Victories
- Defeats
- Winning percentage

▲ Federer examines the Wimbledon trophy with his then coach Tony Roche.

looked in any way fallible. 'As well as playing tennis that was so, so beautiful to watch, Roger was also so, so dominant,' Toni Nadal added.

It was remarkable how quickly everything came together for Federer after winning the 2003 Wimbledon title. By the end of the following January, victory over Juan Carlos Ferrero in the semi-finals of the Australian Open propelled Federer to the world number one ranking for the first time. After beating Marat Safin in the final, Federer received this compliment from the Russian: 'I've just lost to a magician.' And then this from the watching John McEnroe: 'Roger might just be the smoothest, most talented player I've ever set eyes on.' More success followed that year at Wimbledon and the US Open as he became the first man since Mats Wilander in 1988 to win three majors in a season. Federer's only defeat at the 2004 Slams came against Brazilian Gustavo Kuerten in the third round of the French Open.

As Federer's career accelerated, so did discussions within the sport's chattering classes. Only a year and a half earlier there had been doubts about Federer. But before the start of the 2005 season the arguments had been turned on their heads and the debate was about whether he could accomplish the calendar-year Grand Slam. No man had achieved that since Rod Laver in 1969. In the days before the 2005 Australian Open, when the thought was put to Federer, he laughed. 'I find it funny when people say this as it's such an incredible thing to do and people seem to think that it will be easy. If you look at history you will see that a calendar Grand Slam is almost impossible to achieve. But, of course, if it happens I'll be the happiest man in the world.'

Such is Laver's record and aura as the only man to achieve that calendar-year Grand Slam twice, that Andy Roddick says John McEnroe behaves around the Australian like a teenage girl would in the front row of a Justin Bieber concert. Pre-Federer, Laver was regarded by many as 'The Greatest'. But Laver himself was so taken by the level of Federer's tennis during the 2004 season that he suggested he would be 'honoured to even be compared to Roger'. At that stage, Federer had won 'only' four Grand Slams, but already Laver was speaking about him as 'an unbelievable talent' who 'could be the greatest tennis player of all time'. Federer said: 'Someone showed me what Laver had said and I couldn't stop smiling when I read it. I was stunned. It was incredibly nice for someone of that stature, with that incredible record, to be saying such nice things about me.'

As it transpired, Federer's 2005 attempt at the calendar Grand Slam did not even go beyond the semi-finals of the Australian Open, where he lost to Marat Safin. He had a match point against the Russian, but instead of tracking back after a lob and playing a regular shot, which he had time to do, he took the riskier option of a tweener. He hit the ball into the net. That year Federer would win two majors, Wimbledon and the US Open, taking him up to six Grand Slams. That was a significant number because it put him level with two of his idols, Stefan Edberg and Boris Becker. It was becoming increasingly clear that Federer was driven by his place in history. He once said: 'I know I have to live for tennis. I mustn't get injured and I have to stay healthy. I'm not going to be the best player in the world by fooling around. I have to be professional and serious, and stay that way for a long time. That's the difference between the legends and those who are just good players – legends are capable of keeping it going for a long time. That's what I want to achieve, to become a legend.'

Given what Federer had already accomplished, you might say he had already become a legend. That status was only enhanced during the 2006 and 2007 seasons, the years when he came closest to perfection at the Slams. In both years he was champion at the Australian Open, Wimbledon and the US Open, and he made it to the final of the French Open, where he was blocked by Nadal. Still, Nadal could not yet challenge Federer consistently on the other surfaces, which is why Federer was able to achieve the numbers he did during those years. The highest season-long winning percentage of Federer's career was in 2005, when he won 95.3 per cent of his matches, comprising eighty-one victories and four defeats. In 2006, his winning percentage, after ninety-two victories and five defeats, was 94.8. His next best year was 2004, when he won 92.5 per cent of his matches, with seventy-four victories and six defeats.

When Federer dropped a set, it was a news story. 'I don't think you could pick out one match and say that was Roger's greatest performance, or pick out one particular tournament from those years, it was just a whole body of work,' Pete Sampras said. 'He dominated the game during those years. He didn't feel threatened by any of the other players because he was just so much better than anyone else. When Roger wasn't playing well he still found a way to win. He was so consistent, so dominant, and he stayed healthy during that time. There was no one out there who could push him.'

Mats Wilander, winner of seven Grand Slams, believes Federer should be judged primarily by his record against members of his own generation, and in particular against Andy Roddick. Born in 1981, Federer is five years older than Nadal, a child of 1986, and six years the senior of Novak Djokovic and Andy Murray, both born in 1987. The other three members of the Big Four are not from the same generation as Federer. Roddick, born in 1982, and a year younger than Federer, most certainly is. 'There should be much more focus on Roger's rivalry with Roddick because that rivalry played out when Roger was in his prime and when Roddick was in his prime. Against his generation of players, so against those [born] within one or two years of him, he had no problems at all, none, like they hardly ever beat him. His record against those guys, and especially against Roddick, was phenomenal,' Wilander said. 'The fact he is so good that he can float into a different generation – Djokovic, Nadal and Murray – and still be competitive, that's incredible. You're not supposed to be so competitive against players who are five or six years younger than you.'

While Roddick was good enough to win a Grand Slam and hold the number one ranking, he could not stay with Federer. All but three of their twenty-four meetings ended with the words from the umpire's chair: 'Game, set and match, Roger Federer.' On all four occasions they contested a Grand Slam final, Federer was the victor. But it was the manner of Federer's victories over Roddick, and not just the results themselves, that made this rivalry so lopsided that it almost became a non-rivalry. Never was Federer's superiority over Roddick more apparent than during the semi-finals of the 2007 Australian Open. Roddick, who had sounded so confident beforehand, won only six games. He said: 'It was frustrating; it was miserable; it sucked; it was terrible. Besides that, it was fine.' Federer surprised himself with his performance: 'It was just unreal. I've had good matches before, but I've never almost destroyed somebody.'

But maybe there was one match against Roddick when Federer exceeded even that performance at Melbourne Park. And, naturally, it came on the grass of the All England Club, as nowhere has Federer been more consistently brilliant than at Wimbledon.

●

Bjorn Borg says his bond with Roger Federer goes back much further than you might imagine: as far into the past as the 2001 Wimbledon Championships, in fact. That summer, there appeared to be a strong possibility that Borg would lose his status as the only man to have won five successive titles on the lawns. The reason was Pete Sampras, who had won the previous four Championships, and was heavily favoured to score a fifth. The Ice Borg, so calm during his playing days when winning those titles between 1976 and 1980, was perhaps melting a little when following the early rounds from London in 2001, as Sampras moved into the last sixteen. It was not without some turbulence, though, and Sampras needed five sets to see off British wild card Barry Cowan. However, so thrilled was Borg at Federer's fourth-round victory over Sampras, the Swede tracked down a number for Federer and called him. In part it was to pass on his congratulations, but mostly to thank him for protecting his record.

Such was the affection that Borg ended up having for Federer that he did not seem to mind when Federer himself threatened to eclipse him. Not long after Federer defeated Nadal in the 2006 final, to bring up his fourth successive title, Federer and Borg had a practice session in Dubai which the Scandinavian would later describe as 'a beautiful moment'. Federer instigated it, and he was astounded by how well Borg struck the ball, to the extent that he thought he could use him as a regular practice partner. 'Borg's backhand is just the same,' Federer said, 'just like in the videos from the old days.' The next summer, when

▶ OVERLEAF
Federer plays
Agassi in the
2005 US Open
final.

BORG SAID HE SAW
PLENTY OF HIMSELF IN
FEDERER, NOT LEAST IN
THE WAY THEY CARRIED
THEMSELVES ON COURT.
'WE'RE VERY SIMILAR IN
THE WAY ROGER DOESN'T
SHOW HIS EMOTIONS
EITHER. HE DOESN'T LET
IT ALL OUT.'

Federer was playing for that fifth successive title, Borg attended his 'holy place' for only the second time since he was beaten in the 1981 final. The other time was for the millennium parade of champions, an event he had felt obliged to attend. This time it was his decision alone to sit in the front row of the Royal Box.

Federer has never been ruled by superstition as Borg was at Wimbledon. Borg insisted on staying in the same hotel, using the same locker, sitting on the same chair, having the same number of towels at his disposal, and abstaining from shaving and sex until he won the title or was removed from the draw. But Borg said he saw plenty of himself in Federer, not least in the way they carried themselves on court. 'We're very similar in the way Roger doesn't show his emotions either. He doesn't let it all out. Of course, he has feelings and emotions, just like every other human being, it's just that he doesn't like to show them in the stadium. I know how much he cares, but on the court he's a cool guy.' One of the greatest tests of Federer's mental resolve and emotional control came when he played Nadal in the Wimbledon final, in front of the former champion he called 'a living legend'.

Much of Federer's tennis life can be refracted through the green-and-purple prism of the All England Club. It is the Grand Slam tournament with which Federer is most strongly associated. In the beginning, when he was not hitting a ball against the garage wall or the kitchen cupboards of the family home, Federer played his tennis on clay. So before he was anything, he was a clay-courter. And yet, despite those dusty early years, it is grass that suits Federer's attacking game best, giving him more reward for his shots. He has always liked the feel and the sound of a grass court. What is more, much of what Wimbledon stands for – the upholding of traditions, the reserve, the pursuit of excellence – align closely with Federer's view of the tennis world.

It was on Wimbledon's grass, in the summer of 1998, that Federer won his only junior Grand Slam title. Such were his nerves before the first round that he thought the net looked ridiculously, unlawfully high and he asked the umpire to check the height was correct. Of course, it was. This was Wimbledon, after all. But being junior champion at the All England Club is not always reliable evidence of future success in the senior competition. Before Federer, only a small number of players – Borg, Stefan Edberg and Pat Cash

THE CHAMPIONSHIPS

'S SINGLES

1953	V. Seixas
1954	J. Drobny
1955	T. Trabert
1956	L. A. Hoad

▲ Borg and
Federer are the
only men to have
won five
consecutive
Wimbledon titles.

– had been both boys' and men's champions. A much stronger indicator of
Federer's aptitude for lawn tennis came three years later in the senior
tournament when he beat Sampras. And after he won his first senior title in
2003 there was no stopping him. The next two summers he defeated Roddick
in the final. The 2004 final is memorable for Roddick's post-match quote about
Federer: 'I threw the kitchen sink at Roger, but he went to the bathroom and
got the tub.' Such was Federer's performance in the 2005 final, a much more
one-sided encounter than the summer before, there is reason to think it was
the finest one-off performance of his career. It was also perhaps the greatest
tennis played in a Wimbledon final, better even than when Sampras played
Andre Agassi in 1999. Federer's father, Robert, had not been present to watch
his son's first two Wimbledon titles. Someone, he said, had to stay home in
Switzerland to feed the cat. But thankfully Federer senior did not miss that
2005 final.

    The first of Federer's three consecutive Wimbledon finals against Nadal, in
2006, went to four sets. The following year Federer played his first five-set
match at the All England Club since becoming a Wimbledon champion. The
closeness of the match, along with the pressure Federer had felt in attempting
to equal Borg's five titles in a row, led to one of the most emotional

WINNING A MAJOR WITHOUT DROPPING A SET ALL TOURNAMENT

100%

Roger Federer
2007 Australian Open
2017 Wimbledon

100%

100%

Ken Rosewall
1971 Australian Open

Ilie Năstase
1973 French Open

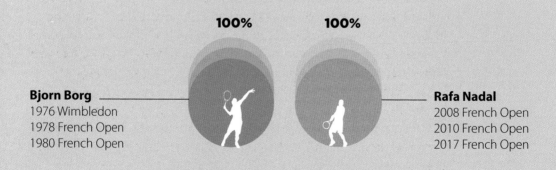

100%

100%

Bjorn Borg
1976 Wimbledon
1978 French Open
1980 French Open

Rafa Nadal
2008 French Open
2010 French Open
2017 French Open

celebrations of his career. The moment victory was secured Federer threw himself back and before he had even hit the grass tears appeared in his eyes. As he pulled himself to his feet, and embraced Nadal at the net, he continued to cry. There were even more tears after he sat down on his chair. Federer, who made a point during his on-court remarks of thanking Borg for being there, met the former champion backstage for a 'Swedish hug'. Federer would win more Wimbledon titles, but never again would he be as dominant a grass-court figure as he was that day.

No one else has won five successive titles at two different Grand Slams, and no one else has been US Open champion five seasons in a row. Such was Federer's dominance in New York that the sight of him holding up the trophy at the Arthur Ashe Stadium became a part of summer. There were other signs that this player from a sleepy town on the Rhine had the Big Apple under his control: some years the fleet of official cars and mini-buses taking the players from their downtown hotels to Flushing Meadows would have his image on the side. Back in Manhattan, Federer would stay in a suite named in his honour, resting his head on pillow-cases with the R.F. monogram. The suite, which is available outside the tournament dates at a cost of thousands of dollars a night, also contains a plaque commemorating his achievements.

The US Open has a rawness about it that the other Slams lack, but this urbane, elegant European brought order to the place with his five-year run, starting in 2004. Some of Federer's best performances came in New York finals, most notably when he claimed two 'bagel' 6–0 sets in the 2004 final against Lleyton Hewitt, or when he beat Andre Agassi in four sets in the 2005 final. Before then, only two other men in the modern era, namely Jimmy Connors and Pete Sampras, had won five US Open titles, though not in a row. In the 2006 final Connors had the hope, albeit indirectly, that he could block Federer from gathering another title as he was coaching Roddick, the finalist that year. But Federer just kept on winning, as he did the following summer against Novak Djokovic. 'How long is this run going to last?' Federer kept on asking himself. The answer was one more year. He would beat Andy Murray in the 2008 final, and though he would establish a two-sets-to-one lead in his sixth successive New York final in 2009, it was Argentine Juan Martín del Potro who took the title.

Something similar happened on the other side of the world. If you believe what Marat Safin said after the 2004 Australian Open, there was something magical about Federer's tennis. But if Federer's tennis was at a high level in 2006, when he defeated the Greek–Cypriot Marcos Baghdatis in the final, the following year no one could touch him at Melbourne Park. It was not just that he defeated Fernando González, a Chilean with a 'Gonzo' forehand, in three sets in the final, but he did not drop a set in the entire tournament. That had not happened at a Grand Slam since Borg's run to the 1980 French Open title. That was also the Australian Open when Federer marmalised Roddick in the semi-finals. 'I felt so relaxed during the tournament,' Federer disclosed, 'it was a joke.'

●

▼ Federer on the practice court with Tony Roche.

'I'm number one, and you can't get ranked higher than one so, OK, now what? What do I do now?' That, Paul Annacone revealed, was the question Roger Federer was constantly trying to address during his 300-plus weeks at the top of the rankings. 'The folks who just touch the world number one ranking, they've achieved something pretty amazing,' Annacone said. 'But the people

who stay there for a long time, that's spectacular.' Annacone should know as he has coached two men who have accomplished the 'spectacular' in tennis: Pete Sampras (286 weeks as number one) and Federer. It was while he was collaborating with Annacone that Federer had the third of his three stretches at the head of the rankings: his triumph at the 2012 Wimbledon Championships put him back as number one for seventeen weeks. Combined with his first run at the top of 237 weeks, from 2004 to 2008, and then the forty-eight weeks that began after winning the 2009 Wimbledon title, Federer has spent a total of 302 weeks at the summit of the men's game.

'Oh my God, I made it to number one,' Federer said after beating Spain's Juan Carlos Ferrero in the semi-finals of the 2004 Australian Open. That, according to Annacone, was the easy part. 'I remember Pete telling me once that it's way harder to stay there than it is to get there, as you have to figure out your evolution once you have achieved being number one. It's not that you don't enjoy the accomplishment of being number one, but you have to consider why you're playing and how you define yourself as a tennis player. So you're thinking, "What do I do? Is it now about winning tournaments? Or solely about winning majors?" Players like Pete and Roger need to have a clear idea of what they want to do next.'

Motivation, though, hardly seemed to be a problem for Federer. He finished as the year-end number one on five occasions, one fewer than Sampras. Federer cared deeply about being number one: for years one of his top priorities for the season ahead was to hold on to that ranking. Yet before the start of the 2005 tennis campaign, and after a successful year that included three Grand Slam titles, he was frustrated that he had not had enough time to work on his game. 'The past year has been impossible. I went from tournament to tournament to tournament, and then I had to rest, so I didn't feel as though I had as much time on the practice court as I would have wanted. Practice is a must. If you don't practise, you won't improve. You'll stay in the same place and the other players will catch you up. I'm determined to stay ahead of the rest.'

Only a privileged few get into triple figures for consecutive weeks at number one. Jimmy Connors held office for 160 weeks in a row, Ivan Lendl for 157, and Sampras for 102. Federer's 237 weeks trumps them all. 'It's very hard being the world number one for a long time,' Sampras said. 'I don't think it's humanly possible to keep that up for more than a few years. Eventually you're going to have a let-down. Being number one is something you carry with you from tournament to tournament. You go to a tournament and you're dealing with a lot more than the other guys. You're dealing with the expectations and the demands and the media. It takes it out of you. The guy who is ranked number twenty, all he is focused on is his tennis. It's an individual sport so you can't deflect anything. You can't hide at any time. It's on you. Being number one is an all-year-long commitment, and the tennis season is a long year.'

According to Annacone, to thrive as the world number one, a player must be able to 'manage all the expectations of that position, and at the same time make sure that his career trajectory is going in the right way'. 'A lot of it, for Roger and for Pete, has been about the expectations and the landscape around them. The better you are, the greater the expectation, both external and internal. The people I've worked with, they tend to be their own harshest critics anyway and expect to win every tournament they enter. With greatness, that's how it is. You tend to be your own barometer.' Annacone disclosed that Federer and Sampras found different ways of coping. 'Pete was always much more insular. He kept things small and more controlled. The group around him was smaller. It was a much more controlled environment. Roger travels with four kids now. He has a big team. He is much more involved in external, off-the-court stuff. He has a lot more sponsors. He is a global ambassador. Roger does things very differently because he chooses to,' Annacone said. 'Pete did it the way he needed to do it to be successful and to stay clear about what his priorities were. The biggest one was trying to win as many major titles as possible. I think Pete dealt with it fine because he preferred to live a quieter life. In that regard Roger doesn't mind the noise and all the distractions. He seems to handle that very well.'

Ultimately, what enabled Federer to spend all those weeks at number one was his desire to compete. 'Being ranked number one for more than three hundred weeks, that's testimony to how much he enjoys playing, week in and week out. To see the expression on his face when he wins a smaller tournament, that shows just how much he loves to play and to win,' Annacone said. As Federer once exclaimed: 'It's fantastic – I recommend it to everybody.'

The first time Federer lost the top ranking, when he was deposed by Rafa Nadal in the summer of 2008, was not easy to take. He did not like it one bit when a stadium announcer introduced him as the world number two. That

▲ Federer 'loves to play and to win'.

did not seem right. So he worked his way back. He had two more runs at the apex, and there was almost another. When Federer arrived at the 2014 season-ending tournament in London, marking his first year with Stefan Edberg as coach, there was a chance he could end the year as number one. In the end, though, he could not force himself above Novak Djokovic. 'Roger is no longer driven by wanting to be number one again. It's no longer a priority,' Annacone said. 'A few years ago, when we were together, he did want to see if he could get back to number one and to win a Slam, and he did that. But now it's about trying to enjoy his career, and the different segments of it, because at his age he's not going to play thirty tournaments a year and chase a ranking. It's about making sure he plays well at the right time, which of course includes at the majors.'

7

THE
BALLERINA
AGAINST
THE BOXER

'WIMBLEDON IS JUST UNBELIEVABLE, IT'S WHERE ALL THE TRADITIONS OF TENNIS COME FROM, AND THIS MATCH WAS BETWEEN TWO SUCH GREAT PLAYERS, WHO WERE RANKED ONE AND TWO AT THE TIME. THERE WAS DARKNESS, RAIN, DRAMA, AND INCREDIBLE TENNIS.'

'Bloody hell,' Pascal Maria, the Frenchman sitting in the umpire's chair for the 2008 Wimbledon final, thought to himself as Roger Federer played the backhand pass of his life. As Maria recalled it, the Centre Court crowd, normally the most restrained in tennis, 'went ballistic'. Federer's backhand down the line, with Rafa Nadal all over the net, would have been a fine piece of skill at any time, but this one was executed when he had a championship point against him. Could anyone other than Federer have played that shot in that moment? So many times during Federer's career he has been brave with his choices, and what better example than this. Federer's backhand enabled the match to become an instant and enduring classic. To put it into context, the final had looked very straightforward when Nadal led by two sets to love. But Federer's moment of brilliance helped take it to a fifth set and deeper still into the evening gloom and murk. 'What luck,' Maria thought to himself, 'that I was assigned this match.' As he said later: 'Wimbledon is just unbelievable, it's where all the traditions of tennis come from, and this match was between two such great players, who were ranked one and two at the time. There was darkness, rain, drama, and incredible tennis.'

There is extraordinary hyperbole in the immediate aftermath of almost every Wimbledon final, but the snap analysis on television and radio after Nadal and Federer's five-setter – that this was the greatest match in the history of the sport – still holds. Like watching an angel fall was how one observer inside Centre Court saw it. Federer had been attempting to win an unprecedented sixth consecutive Wimbledon title, while Nadal's aim had been to hold the trophy for the first time, and demonstrate that he was much

▶ Nadal comforts his rival after the 2009 Australian Open final.

more than just a clay-courter. Victory would also make Nadal the first man since Bjorn Borg in 1980 to win the European Slams in the same summer. Adding to a drama that ran for four hours and forty-eight minutes' playing time was the weather. There had already been two interruptions. During one of them, according to an account by the American tennis writer Jon Wertheim, Federer's future wife, Mirka, intercepted the defending champion backstage and reminded him: *'You are Roger Federer.'*

The match did not finish until 9.17 p.m., by which time the numbers on the scoreboard were glowing, and it had become increasingly difficult for the players to pick out the ball. For the armchair audience it looked bright enough, but they were watching a picture that had been enhanced for television. Inside Centre Court the gloom was real enough. 'I believe that had the final set reached eight–all, the match would have been suspended, and we would have returned the next day,' Maria disclosed. 'But, as it turned out, Nadal took that set 9–7 and it was all over that day.' Federer was extremely upset about playing in the gloom. 'It bothers me a lot and it is hard to accept that the world's most important tennis match took place in a light where it was practically impossible to play.' Federer said he had barely been able to make out Nadal's face. And if Federer had not suffered from glandular fever, or mononucleosis, at the start of that year, costing him twenty training days and weakening his body, would he have won this final?

Still, for all the distress and disappointment that Federer felt after his run was ended, in time he came to appreciate that the final, which his father called 'a hell of a match, a hell of a catfight', has done much to promote the sport. Their intense encounters helped make Federer versus Nadal the greatest rivalry men's tennis has known, above John McEnroe and Bjorn Borg or Pete Sampras and Andre Agassi or McEnroe and Jimmy Connors. But no match will ever do as much for tennis as that dank, dark evening on Centre Court. 'Their rivalry has been a great thing for the sport. Their personalities are different but both have good images for tennis,' Toni Nadal said. 'For the spectator, Roger is a wonderful player. He won all those Grand Slams, was number one for so many weeks, and you might say that he is the greatest tennis player of all time. With Roger and Rafa, here are two guys who play in a completely different ways – one has wonderful technique and the other has passion and runs so fast. Roger and Rafa made some wonderful finals together, and none so great as that 2008 Wimbledon final.'

▲ Federer and
Nadal's rivalry
took the sport to
new heights.

▶ OVERLEAF
The 2008
Wimbledon final,
between Federer
and Nadal, was
the greatest
match of all time..

Toni Nadal has a theory about his nephew, Federer and what might be termed the quest for greatness. 'They exhausted each other,' he said. Such was the intensity of their rivalry, Toni said, that Nadal and Federer burned through great amounts of mental and physical energy. But Toni was also talking about how the pair depleted each other's reserves of talent. In every way both had nothing more to give. They had reached the limits of what they, or any other tennis players, could achieve. With Nadal around, there were no what-ifs for Federer. He was the best he could possibly be.

Toni Nadal's analysis runs counter to the thoughts of some of Federer's most committed supporters. A popular take among some of those who wear R.F.-logoed baseball caps is that Nadal's muscular approach, all biceps and lefty, whippy forehands, was somehow an intrusion on Federer's genius. My preference is for the Toni Nadal thesis. Perhaps the best way of thinking about Nadal's part in the Federer story, and he is one of the central characters, is that he enhanced Federer's brilliance rather than detracted from it. Nadal has been the greatest challenge of Federer's life. Without Nadal, Federer would have

▲ Federer congratulates Nadal on his victory.

been a worse tennis player, and not just because it was Nadal who compelled Federer to upgrade his backhand. Only Nadal could have provoked, challenged and inspired Federer to produce such an astonishing level of tennis in the 2017 Australian Open final, with the Swiss playing eyeballs-out to take the last five games of the match. 'They were already on a high level, but every day – day after day after day – they were pushing to get higher and higher, and to get that little bit better, and so they reached their limits,' Toni Nadal said. 'They could not have done any more.'

The first meeting of Federer and Nadal, amid the muggy heat, wind and splayed palm trees of Miami, in the spring of 2004, had not been a fair fight. The conditions there make it the kind of tournament you should not play if there is any doubt about your physical fitness. Federer had thought about withdrawing because of illness, but in the end decided to play. He would lose early on to Nadal, and in straight sets. They would meet again in Miami the following spring, this time in the final, and Federer came from two sets down for victory. But it was their match in the 2006 clay-court final in Rome – a five-set, five-hour humdinger, which Nadal won – that alerted the wider sporting world that, for the first time, Federer had a rival who could trouble him, even if at that stage it was only consistently on clay. It was a couple of years before this supposed 'dirt-baller' encroached on Federer's lawn with that 2008 victory.

The boxer to Federer's ballerina, the *New Yorker* magazine once observed of Nadal. But Nadal's usefulness went way beyond stress-testing Federer's technique, resolve and ambition. He also provided a great story. How badly did Federer need Nadal? Without Nadal, the Federer narrative would have lacked dramatic tension. Without Nadal, where was the jeopardy? Naturally, it would have enhanced Federer's claims for true greatness if he had won all four majors in a year, which he would surely have done, and at least once, had Nadal not been on the scene. But there would have been a cost to Federer. Would the tennis public have been as entertained, and as engaged, without Nadal? Would the galleries have invested so much in Federer's pursuit of his first French Open title, which would complete his career Grand Slam, if Nadal had not blocked him for so many years? The public want to see genius, but they prefer to see it challenged, pushed, coerced. How does genius deal with adversity, such as the 'brutal' defeat to Nadal in the 2008 French Open final when Federer won only four games? Without a dramatic arc, a story is not much of a tale. Perhaps, as Toni Nadal suggested, his nephew really was one of the best things that ever happened to Federer.

●

MOST TITLES FEDERER WON IN A YEAR

| | Titles won | 5 | 10 |

▲ Federer's
victory at Roland
Garros in 2009
completed his
Career Grand
Slam.

The men's singles final at Roland Garros can always be expected to bring out an emotional response in Rafa Nadal. And, once again, tears appeared in his eyes at the conclusion of the 2009 French Open. This time, though, the tears were not for himself, but for the man he had defeated in the previous year's final for the loss of just four games. On this occasion Nadal was not the one raising great, orange-red clouds of dust in Paris or coming under the scrutiny of the spider-cam on Court Philippe Chatrier. Instead he was at home in Majorca watching on television. Earlier in the fortnight Nadal had experienced defeat at Roland Garros for the first time, with a fourth-round loss to Robin Söderling, a Swede with a mighty slap of a forehand. Only later was the full extent of Nadal's knee problem discovered, and how he had been troubled at the time by difficulties in his parents' marriage. Now, on the day of the final, Nadal was moved by what he was watching as Federer defeated Söderling to win the French Open for the first time and become a member of the most elite club in tennis, those who have completed the Career Grand Slam. Only years later would Nadal speak publicly about those tears of happiness for his greatest rival. Nadal's reaction told you plenty about his generosity of spirit and the warmth of the relationship he has with Federer. But it also said much

▲ Roger Federer receives *La Coupe des Mousquetaires* from Andre Agassi.

about how Federer's pursuit of La Coupe des Mousquetaires – The Musketeers' Cup – had become an obsession into which everybody in the sport, almost without exception, had bought.

There was absolutely no need to tell Nadal how badly Federer had been wanting to win the French Open. For years he had seen that ambition up close, from just over the net, and had then vaporised it, first in the 2005 semi-final, and then in the 2006, 2007 and 2008 finals. It was Nadal, and Nadal alone, who had made a Federer victory in Paris all the more meaningful. For years Federer had been the second best clay-courter in the world. There was no shame in being number two when the man he trailed was the greatest force on clay the sport had seen. But the debate was whether it was Federer's destiny never to conquer France. Some would suggest that clay-court tennis is a sport within a sport. There is a whole tribe of tennis greats – among them Pete Sampras, John McEnroe, Boris Becker and Stefan Edberg – who did not win the French Open. Would Federer join them, or could he join Fred Perry, Don Budge, Roy Emerson, Rod Laver and

NADAL WAS MOVED BY WHAT HE WAS WATCHING AS FEDERER DEFEATED SÖDERLING TO WIN THE FRENCH OPEN FOR THE FIRST TIME AND BECOME A MEMBER OF THE MOST ELITE CLUB IN TENNIS, THOSE WHO HAVE COMPLETED THE CAREER GRAND SLAM.

A SELECTION OF FEDERER'S GREATEST RECORDS

Roger Federer was twenty-seven years old when he completed the Career Grand Slam with his victory at the 2009 French Open. At the time, Federer was the sixth man to achieve this feat, but Rafa Nadal joined the club by winning the 2010 US Open, and Novak Djokovic completed his set with victory at the 2016 French Open. Here are the ages at which players achieved the Career Grand Slam:

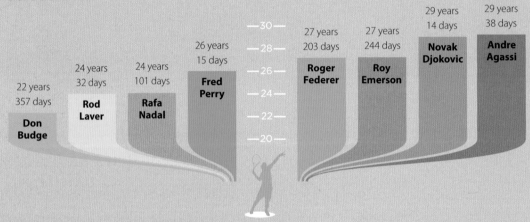

22 years
357 days
Don Budge

24 years
32 days
Rod Laver

24 years
101 days
Rafa Nadal

26 years
15 days
Fred Perry

27 years
203 days
Roger Federer

27 years
244 days
Roy Emerson

29 years
14 days
Novak Djokovic

29 years
38 days
Andre Agassi

FEDERER'S RECORDS FOR CONSECUTIVE GRAND SLAM QUARTER-FINALS, SEMI-FINALS AND FINALS

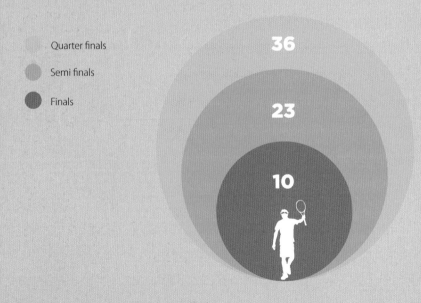

Quarter finals

Semi finals

Finals

36

23

10

Roger Federer has the record for the greatest number of weeks at world number one (302) and also for the longest streak of consecutive weeks at the top (237)

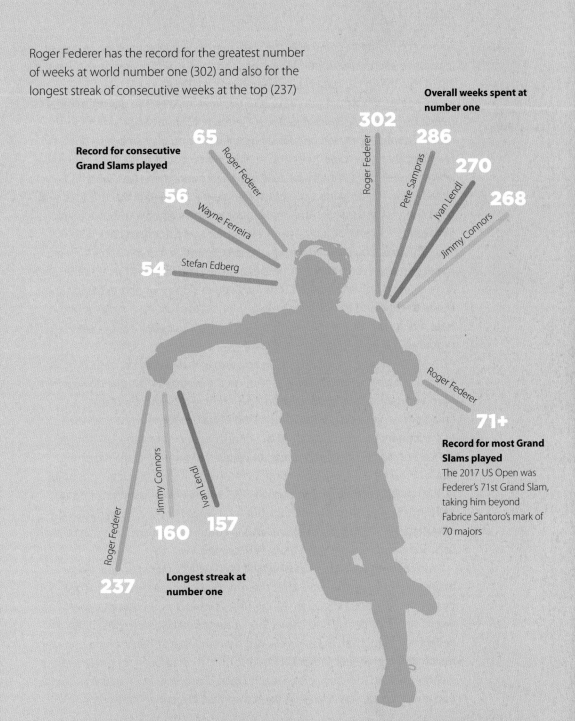

Overall weeks spent at number one

302 Roger Federer
286 Pete Sampras
270 Ivan Lendl
268 Jimmy Connors

Record for consecutive Grand Slams played

65 Roger Federer
56 Wayne Ferreira
54 Stefan Edberg

Roger Federer

71+

Record for most Grand Slams played
The 2017 US Open was Federer's 71st Grand Slam, taking him beyond Fabrice Santoro's mark of 70 majors

Roger Federer
Jimmy Connors
Ivan Lendl

160
157

237

Longest streak at number one

▼ OVERLEAF
Federer's triumph
in the 2009
Wimbledon final
took him to a
record fifteen
Grand Slams.

Andre Agassi and become only the sixth man to win all four of the majors at least once each? Also under discussion at the time: did Federer need a French Open to confirm his status as The Greatest of All Time?

Federer almost did not make it to the final in 2009. The day after Nadal's defeat by Söderling, Federer had met Germany's Tommy Haas in the fourth round. During the match he found himself having to play an inside-out forehand that now looks to be the most important shot of his life. Federer was down a break point. If he missed with this forehand, then Haas, who had already won the opening two sets, would take a 5–3 lead in the third set, and be serving for the match. After making room for the shot with some quick footwork, Federer took a big swing. He certainly did not hold back with the shot. This was a ball loaded with pace, spin, ambition, maybe a smidgen of hope, perhaps even a touch of desperation, and no little historical significance. A great feeling of relief surged through Federer's body when the ball bounced inside the line and through for a clean winner. 'You just have to tip your hat,' Haas would say later of Federer's precise, powerful stroke, the shot that propelled the Swiss to a five-set victory.

On he went through the draw, and into a final staged on one of those soggy Paris days when it seems as though the surface is just one downpour from turning Roland Garros to mud. The whirling, swirling wind also could not be ignored. The conditions did not allow for the most polished of performances, and neither did the unnerving incident when an intruder jumped on to the court and made for Federer, trying to place a hat on his head. In the time it took for security to intervene, it was difficult not to think of the horrific episode in Hamburg in 1993 when a man plunged a boning knife into Monica Seles's back. Still, but for a wobble in concentration in the minutes after the incident, Federer was in control, and would win in straight sets. Soon Nadal would be in tears. Federer, too.

In the process Federer put himself level with Sampras on fourteen majors, less than seven years after the American had completed his collection by winning the 2002 US Open. At the time it looked as though that mark would stand for decades to come. But, understandably, more was made of Federer's first triumph in Paris. Few had doubted that Federer would one day match and then equal Sampras's figure, but there had been scepticism about whether he had it in him to be French Open champion. Now all those doubts had disappeared. 'It would have been a crime if Roger had never won this

LONGEST WINNING STREAK

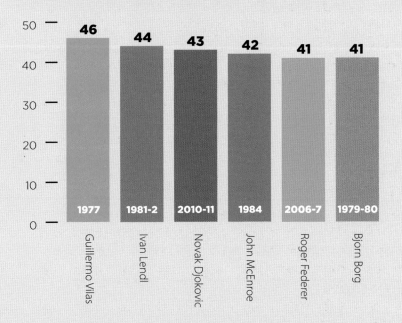

46	**44**	**43**	**42**	**41**	**41**
1977	1981-2	2010-11	1984	2006-7	1979-80
Guillermo Vilas	Ivan Lendl	Novak Djokovic	John McEnroe	Roger Federer	Bjorn Borg

YEAR-END NUMBER ONE

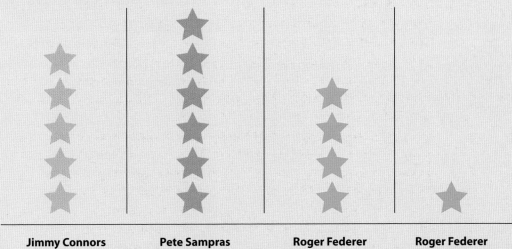

Jimmy Connors
1974–75

Pete Sampras
1993–98

Roger Federer
2004–7

Roger Federer
2009

tournament,' Agassi said after presenting him with the trophy. 'It was destiny, I guess, in many respects. Roger has earned his place, his rightful place, in the game. He's been the second best clay-courter for years, and if it weren't for a kid from Majorca, he would have won a handful of these things.'

Of course, it would have been a stronger storyline if Federer had overcome Nadal in the final. But no asterisk is needed beside Federer's name on the honours board. Any attempt to downgrade Federer's accomplishment should be resisted. A French Open title is a French Open title, and Federer had his full set of majors. To Federer's mind this was the proudest moment of his career, and probably the most important victory. It was not quite true, though, as someone suggested, that this ended twenty-seven years of angst and waiting for Federer. 'Firstly, I never waited twenty-seven years, because twenty-seven years ago I was just born. And my parents never told me, "If you don't win Roland Garros, we take you to an orphanage".' No longer would

▼ Federer and Roddick's match lasted for seventy-seven games, a record for a Wimbledon final.

DOMINANCE AT THE SLAMS

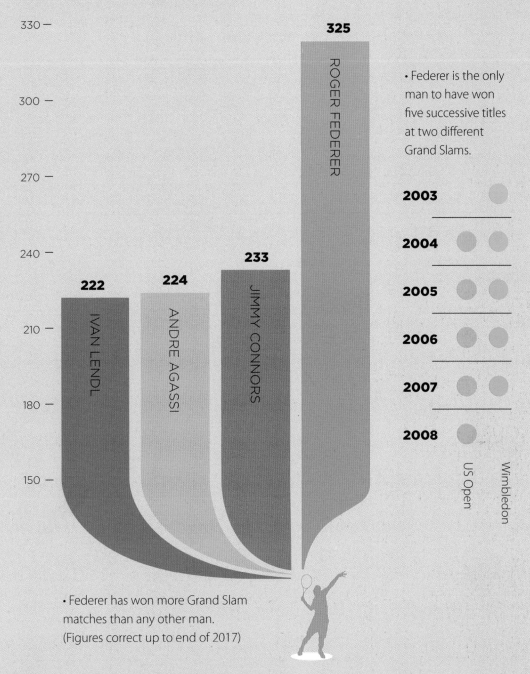

330 —
300 —
270 —
240 —
210 —
180 —
150 —

222 IVAN LENDL

224 ANDRE AGASSI

233 JIMMY CONNORS

325 ROGER FEDERER

• Federer is the only man to have won five successive titles at two different Grand Slams.

2003

2004

2005

2006

2007

2008

US Open

Wimbledon

• Federer has won more Grand Slam matches than any other man.
(Figures correct up to end of 2017)

27 ♛ ROLEX ♛ 4.17

SETS GAMES POINTS

SETS

6 Andy RO

3 Ro r F

CH   G
RO   K
FE   R

AS SAMPRAS FOUND HIS SEAT HE LOOKED ACROSS AT THE SWISS AND GAVE HIM A THUMBS-UP. THAT SAMPRAS WAS THERE AT ALL TOLD YOU MUCH ABOUT HIS GOOD GRACE AND HUMILITY, AND ALSO PLENTY ABOUT THE STRENGTH OF HIS FRIENDSHIP WITH FEDERER.

◄ PREVIOUS
Federer leaps high off the Centre Court grass after becoming the most successful man in tennis history.

Federer have to listen to discussions about why he had not won the elusive major; no longer could anyone suggest that his run of blanks in Paris barred him from true greatness. For the rest of his career, Federer said during his speech, he would be able to play without pressure.

A month later there would be plenty of pressure and stress for Federer on the long afternoon on Wimbledon's Centre Court when he tried to become the first man to win a fifteenth Grand Slam title. Relaxed? Not so much. The final against Andy Roddick would last seventy-seven games, a record for a title-match at the tournament. It cannot have been a relaxing afternoon for Federer's pregnant wife Mirka, who was just days away from giving birth to twin girls. Or for Federer's friend Sampras, sitting in the Royal Box. Such was the significance of the match, Sampras had flown in from Los Angeles on the red-eye to be there, though the American and his wife, the actress Bridgette Wilson, were a few minutes late. As Sampras found his seat he looked across at the Swiss and gave him a thumbs-up. That Sampras was there at all told you much about his good grace and humility, and also plenty about the strength of his friendship with Federer. For all the angst and exertion that had gone into Sampras's collection of Slams, and as much as he had once hoped that his record would stand for a long time, he was happy that the man to eclipse him would be someone he has described as 'the most dominant individual athlete in the history of mankind'. Sampras had felt compelled to travel across the Atlantic for what promised to be 'a big moment'. This was much tighter than the two previous occasions that Federer had encountered Roddick in a Wimbledon final. Such were the small margins that, days later in America, Roddick would open the door to take delivery of a parcel and be forced to listen to the postman's theory on what went wrong. The mistake Roddick had made, according to the mailman, was that he had not changed his sweat-soaked shirt, and so had been weighed down. You can almost picture the thought-bubble forming above Roddick's head as he stood on his doorstep: if only beating Federer was simply a matter of remembering the costume changes. Back in the real world on Centre Court there had been no let-up in tension for four and a quarter hours. 'I had a feeling we would be there all summer long, that they would close the roof, people would sleep all night and wake up, and

PLAYER PROFILES

Comparing Federer's physique with rivals, former greats and athletes from other sports.

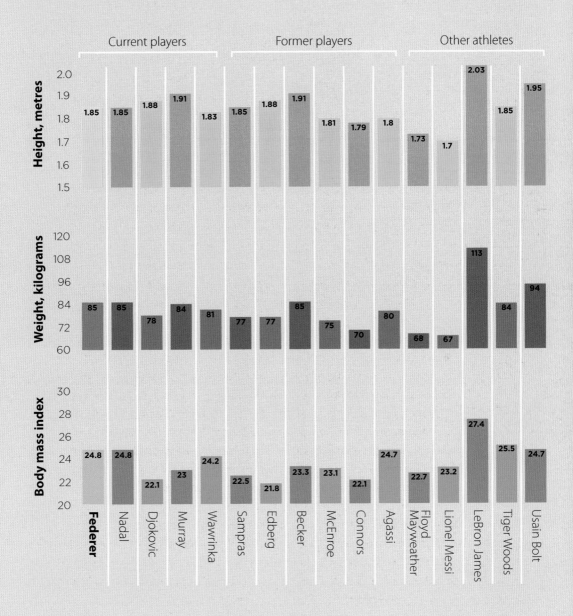

Andy and I would still be there, beards growing, holding serve,' Federer said.

Only in the seventy-seventh and final game did Roddick lose his serve.
Federer had the fifth set 16–14. He also had a sixth Wimbledon title, a fifteenth
Grand Slam and all the accolades. Is there any higher praise at the All England
Club than to be recognised by Sampras, a near-mythical figure at that garden
party, as 'a legend, a stud and an icon'?

●

Great psychological damage has been done during tennis's Belle Époque, and
a good deal of that damage was inflicted by Roger Federer with a game that

some regard as elegant savagery of the highest order. Andy Murray has certainly felt what it is like to be roughed up by Federer. In the words of British sportswriter Oliver Brown: 'Federer has hurt Murray like no other.'

Twice Federer caused Murray to break down, and in the most public of circumstances, standing before a microphone, a crowd of thousands and a global television audience of millions. Twice Federer had messed around with the Murray psyche. Of course, Federer regularly made Andy Roddick rage and cuss and burn up with anger, frustration and unfulfilled ambition. But an angry, frustrated tennis player is one thing, and a weeping player is quite another. There was nothing vindictive about this and Federer certainly had not intended to make Murray cry. It was just that Murray happened to be in the way in the finals of the 2010 Australian Open and 2012 Wimbledon Championships. As a result of those two encounters Murray's collection of Grand Slams was still stuck on zero, while Federer's figure rolled on from fifteen to seventeen. Another illustration of Federer's ability to hurt Murray came on the other side of London, at the 2014 season-ending tournament in Greenwich, where the Swiss conceded just one game in a best-of-three-sets match. Back at Wimbledon, in a semi-final match at the 2015 Championships, Murray had the misfortune to be on the wrong end of Federer's best performance in years.

Still, it would be a mistake to imagine that Federer has had it all his own way against Murray. While Federer has won more of the important matches they have played, including their first Grand Slam final meeting at the 2008 US Open, he has not won them all. Just like Rafa Nadal, Murray has challenged Federer over the years, and so has played his part in making Federer an even better tennis player. For all the pain that came from some of the encounters, there was also a thrill to be had from facing someone he thought of as the greatest player in the sport's history. The first time Murray played Federer, in the final of the Bangkok tournament in 2005, it felt surreal, more like a tennis video game than reality. 'Playing against Roger Federer,' one of Murray's former coaches, Mark Petchey, said, 'is something that Andy has always relished.' On the other side of the net, Federer's admiration for Murray has grown over time, especially after they contested a Grand Slam final for the first time. 'Roger has a lot of respect for the way that Andy plays, and that respect has come gradually,' Britain's John Lloyd, a former Grand Slam finalist, said. 'Roger has come to appreciate what Andy has in his game.'

▲ Federer won his seventeenth Grand Slam by beating Andy Murray in the 2012 Wimbledon final.

Federer's victory in the 2012 Wimbledon final put him level with Pete Sampras on seven titles. Here was confirmation, if confirmation was needed, that there had never been a finer grass-court player. But it also told the tennis world something else. This major came two and a half years after his last Slam, in Australia in 2010, also when beating Murray. Federer was still very much a force in the game, a point backed up by the rankings when he returned to the top of the list the morning after. 'I had tried not to listen to all those people who had been writing Roger off,' Paul Annacone, Federer's coach at the time, said. 'The problem was that people kept referring back to 2004 to 2007, when he was losing about two matches a year. People were comparing two different times. I never doubted that Roger would win another major, but there's no doubt it felt great for Roger, winning that first Slam since 2010. He had worked hard to stay in shape and to get in big matches. For him to come through and do it at Wimbledon, where he had won six times before, that was such a great feeling.'

Within a month Federer would be playing Murray in another final at the All England Club, and a new experience for both of them: a gold-medal match at the Olympics. Some question what tennis is doing in the Olympics, but not Federer. More than once he has had the thrill of carrying his country's flag into the stadium for the Opening Ceremony. From a young age Federer had been interested in the Olympics, inspired by his fellow Swiss Marc Rosset, who won the singles gold medal at Barcelona in 1992. As a nineteen year old, Federer put together a strong run at the 2000 Games in Sydney, before losing in the semi-finals to Tommy Haas. He was then beaten by Frenchman Arnaud Di Pasquale in the play-off for the bronze medal. Four years later, in Athens, Federer went no further than the second round, where he was stopped by Tomáš Berdych, of the Czech Republic. In Beijing his tournament came to an abrupt end in the quarter-finals with a defeat by American James Blake. Reaching the gold-medal match at the London Games had hardly been straightforward, either. He only prevailed with a 19–17 final set in his semi-final against Juan Martín del Potro, yet he was still favoured to beat Murray. What few had anticipated was that Murray would raise his game so significantly that he beat Federer in straight sets. While Federer won the doubles gold in Beijing alongside Stan Wawrinka, the singles title has eluded him.

FEDERER'S RIVALRIES

Percentage of matches won by Federer.

Player	Grass	Hard	Clay	All surfaces
with Rafa Nadal	67%	53%	13%	38%
with Novak Djokovic	33%	48%	50%	49%
with Andy Murray	67%	57%	0%	56%
with Lleyton Hewitt	67%	68%	100%	67%
with Andy Roddick	100%	84%	100%	88%

8

MUSES, COACHES AND QUIET VOICES IN HIS EAR

WHEN FEDERER HIRED IVAN LJUBIČIĆ, IT WAS THE FIRST TIME HE HAD EMPLOYED A COACH WHO HAD ONCE BEEN AN OPPONENT AND REGULAR PRACTICE PARTNER ON THE ATP WORLD TOUR. BUT LJUBIČIĆ WOULDN'T BE FEDERER'S ONLY COACH – HE WAS ASSISTED BY SEVERIN LÜTHI, WHO HAD BEEN ON THE SCENE FOR YEARS.

In the age of the super-coach, during which Andre Agassi, John McEnroe, Ivan Lendl, Boris Becker and Stefan Edberg have sprinkled celebrity stardust over the modern generation, Severin Lüthi has gone quietly about his business. Whether standing at the back of the practice court, or sitting in Roger Federer's guest-box in stadiums around the world, Lüthi has been hiding in plain sight for years. When television directors have cut to Federer's team between points, the camera has sometimes lingered briefly on Lüthi, though few viewers could have told you his name without a caption.

While hiring a famous face has become fashionable, many of the men who have held the world number one ranking, and won multiple Grand Slams and millions of dollars, have not had as much influence and impact on the sport as Lüthi. Yet his ranking as a player peaked at 622 and his career prize-money was $520. If, after working with Federer for a decade, Lüthi barely has a profile to speak of, that is just the way he likes it. As Federer has noted, Lüthi does not much care for 'polishing his reputation' through media appearances, so has not been given the credit he deserves; the coach's only concern is improving Federer's tennis and helping his close friend land as many trophies as possible. One of the few occasions that Lüthi found himself alone in the arc-lights was when he won the Coach of the Year prize at the 2017 Swiss Sports Awards, after which Federer wrote he was 'lucky' to have Lüthi in his team, telling him: 'You've been a rock in my corner for years.'

No one has a better understanding of Federer's game and personality than Lüthi. That knowledge is worth far more than any celebrity status. 'As a coach, he's really valuable to me. He knows my game very well. He knows my practice sessions very well. He knows what I need to work on,' Federer has said.

Federer with his coaches Severin Lüthi and Ivan Ljubičić.

'He knows what makes me happy and sad.'

As the years have passed, Lüthi appears to have made himself even more integral to Federer's tennis life, both for the technical instruction, strategy and encouragement he delivers himself and also for how he sets the overall mood within the team. For the last ten years, Federer has worked with a number of coaches with much more recognisable faces, like Paul Annacone, Edberg and Ivan Ljubičić, yet the ever-present Lüthi has been instrumental in making those partnerships work.

'An underrated force in the game,' is Annacone's assessment. 'Severin is the glue that holds things together. People should probably be speaking about Severin a little more. It's easy for people to gravitate towards big, prominent coaching names and talk about them. Severin doesn't have a huge name, but he plays a huge role. I know that without Severin there, I would have really struggled at the beginning. He really helped to make the transition easy for me, and also easy for Roger. Severin is a wealth of information. He

does a great job and makes an impact.

'He knows Roger better than anyone else. A lot of the value that he brings is the combination of two things: that he knows the game and the person. That means he is able to give Roger very clear instruction and a clear evaluation of what's going on. And then Roger is able to digest that information quickly and adjust as needed, and that's really helpful.'

In the two years Federer worked with Edberg, it was understandable that the Swede attracted media and public attention. As well as being a winner of six Grand Slam titles, Edberg was Federer's childhood idol, which only added to the fascination with their alliance. But then, in December 2015, Federer's collaboration with Edberg ended and he turned to Ljubičić, and once again the focus would be on someone other than Lüthi. Despite that imbalance, the reality was that, for all the credit due to Ljubičić for Federer's 2017 resurgence, Lüthi deserves just the same, if not more, for his work behind the scenes.

●

Why, though, did Roger Federer even need a coach? After all, he had won a bunch of Grand Slam titles without someone in his corner. Some of the greatest tennis of his life had been when he was without a coach, most notably in 2004 when he won three majors. More than any other player operating at the top level, Federer became very self-sufficient during those periods. Indeed, he even booked his own practice courts and hitting-partners. That might sound unremarkable, but you can be sure that others in his situation would not know how to deal with their daily admin.

At those times, perhaps the closest person he had to a coach was whichever I.B.M. employee happened to hand him a sheet of match statistics when he came off court. The whisper in the locker room was that Federer could look at those numbers and then make all the tweaks required for next time. The reality, though, is that he could have done that without the data. He found that after a few matches against an opponent it barely took him a few minutes to decide on a game-plan for their next encounter. So why pay someone to complicate his thinking when he was perfectly capable of 'solving

◀ How much did Federer even need a coach?

SERVE-AND-VOLLEY

Percentage of points during Federer's service games at
Wimbledon that he serve-and-volleyed.

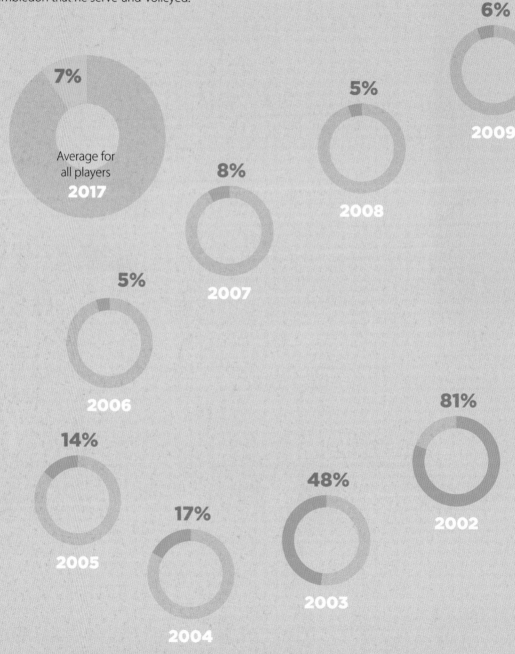

6%
2009

7%

Average for
all players
2017

5%
2008

8%
2007

5%
2006

81%
2002

14%
2005

17%
2004

48%
2003

5%
2010

4%
2011

9%
2012

12%
2013

22%
2014

16%
2015

11%
2016

16%
2017

MUSES, COACHES AND QUIET VOICES IN HIS EAR

EVERYDAY LUX

▲ Federer in conversation with Paul Annacone at the Australian Open.

the riddles', as he put it, on his own? And even when Federer did link up with coaches, they were not with him for the forty weeks a year that Peter Lundgren had been.

Take the partnership with Tony Roche, the Australian former French Open champion, who was getting on for forty years Federer's senior, and who had coached Ivan Lendl and Pat Rafter. 'Partnership' makes it sound a lot firmer and more committed than it really was. It was an 'arrangement', and a loose one at that. On the face of it, this was hugely successful, with Federer winning six Grand Slams in the two and a half years they spent together. Roche, himself a lefty, helped Federer get into the mind of his left-handed rival, Rafa Nadal. But Roche was only with his client around the Grand Slams. Long periods would pass without Federer and Roche communicating, apart from the odd text message from the coach saying, 'Well done' or 'Good luck'. 'It has been too quiet between us,' Federer said when explaining why they split just a fortnight before the 2007 French Open.

Federer's relationship with José Higueras for a chunk of the 2008 season was also part-time. In 2009, Federer had a trial training period in Dubai with Darren Cahill, Peter Carter's old friend. Federer hoped to encourage Cahill to join him on the Tour, but the 'incredibly luring and enticing' offer was declined because Cahill did not want to be away from his young family. Then along came Paul Annacone, who gave Federer more time than Roche and Higueras had, before Stefan Edberg arrived.

●

In the beginning, Roger Federer could not see the appeal of Stefan Edberg. As a tennis-obsessed boy growing up in Teutonic Basel in the 1980s and early 1990s, Federer was fanatical about Boris Becker. He adored the young German's will to win even more than he loved Becker's serve and his spectacular dives across the court. It was plain just how much that strawberry-blond kid cared, just as it was obvious how much a young Federer cared. Even when Federer's friends urged him to support Edberg – 'because he's so cool and so classy' – he still could not appreciate him as others did. Back then Federer had still to master cool and classy. So when Edberg defeated Becker in the 1988 Wimbledon final, and again when they met for the 1990 title, Federer watched the closing moments and prize-giving through eyes full of tears. Only in 1989, when Becker defeated Edberg, the middle meeting of their three successive Wimbledon finals, could Federer sit through an entire broadcast with dry eyes.

When Federer was a little older he came to understand why friends admired Edberg for his more understated, gentlemanly nature, as well as for playing tennis with such aggression and adventure that it bordered on the reckless. Beneath that cool exterior was someone who embraced risk. Edberg, who won the last of his six Grand Slam titles at the 1992 US Open, became the player who provided the greatest inspiration for a pre-teen Federer sitting in front of his television set in Basel.

BUT DID FEDERER EVEN NEED A COACH? AFTER ALL, HAD HE NOT WON A BUNCH OF GRAND SLAMS WITHOUT SOMEONE IN HIS CORNER? SOME OF THE GREATEST TENNIS OF FEDERER'S LIFE HAD BEEN WHEN HE WAS WITHOUT A COACH, MOST NOTABLY IN 2004 WHEN HE WON THREE MAJORS.

The two champions from different eras met in the grandeur of the Waldorf Astoria in midtown Manhattan a few days before the start of the US Open in 2013. The ATP were holding a party to mark forty years of their official rankings, and invited as guests of honour all the players who had been number one. Even though he had a Grand Slam to prepare for, Federer stayed a little later than expected. Here, after all, was an opportunity to connect with an idol. At the time, Federer already had a coach in Paul Annacone. However, a few days later, on the concrete

AT THE NET

Percentage of points won when at the net during the
Grand Slam finals that Federer won.

Success **75%**

Average number of approaches to the net per set

10

Australian Open

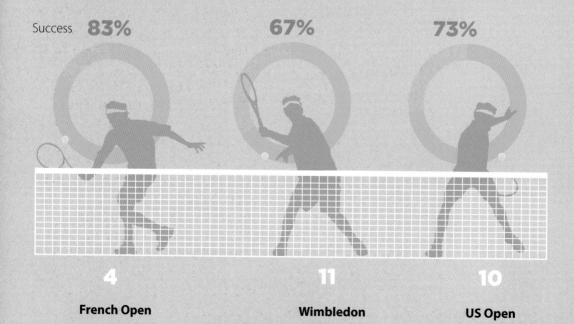

Success **83%**   **67%**   **73%**

4   **11**   **10**

French Open   **Wimbledon**   **US Open**

of Flushing Meadows, Federer lost in the fourth round to Spaniard Tommy Robredo. It was the first time in a decade he had not reached the quarter-finals, and the defeat was another disappointment in a season of frustration. He won only one title all year, the grass-court tournament at Halle in Germany, and did not play in a single Grand Slam final for the first time since 2002. The most excruciating moment during Federer's year, in which he suffered with a bad back, came at Wimbledon when he went out in the second round to Ukraine's Sergiy Stakhovsky. After the straight-sets defeat by Robredo in New York, there were even mutterings outside the Federer camp about retirement.

Two months after that evening at the Waldorf, Federer broke off his partnership with Annacone. It had been a three-year collaboration that plundered only one major, the 2012 Wimbledon title. Edberg, meanwhile, had been living a 'quiet and comfortable life', which included his involvement with an investment firm he co-founded when his playing career ended. He certainly had not been expecting a call from Federer asking him to join his camp. Indeed, he did not have any ambitions to be involved in elite tennis again. Had it been anyone else on the line it is probable that Edberg would have politely declined the offer. But because it was Federer he consulted closely with his family, who supported his decision to join up on a part-time basis. In Edberg's mind he did not feel able to turn down the chance 'to just be around Roger, such a special person on and off the court', especially as he believed he could help. Much of Edberg's focus would be on Federer's volleying.

There is a great solitude, as well as a majesty, to Federer as he moves towards the net and prepares to play a volley. To an extent he shares that isolation with all other tennis players. Anyone who swings a racket is at their most exposed when they venture into the service box. However you play it, whatever your strategies, tennis is a one-on-one gladiatorial game. Yet being at the net, and waiting for your opponent to strike with an attempted pass or lob, reinforces the feeling. Federer, though, flies solo like no other.

As *L'Équipe* observed one morning during the 2015 French Open, Federer is *'un volleyeur solitaire'*. They meant that Federer is that rare creature who embraces coming to the net, who regards it as a key part of his game, unlike those players who only enter the service boxes when there is no other option. Pete Sampras would speak of the lost art of serve-and-volleying as if it was as relevant to the modern world as the fax machine. The American and his cohorts complain that modern racket and string technology has enabled players to stay back on the baseline and 'hit the crap out of the ball'. The old pros lament that the modern generation only come to the net for the pre-match toss of the coin and to shake hands at the end. In every other part of tennis, from serving to groundstrokes, physical conditioning to mental preparation, today's players have pushed the sport to greater heights. Only in the service box has modern tennis regressed.

Even so, there is an outlier who will not be ignored. Federer has gone further than anyone else in trying to keep the art alive. And this has happened when he is in his thirties, at a stage when he is not supposed to be trying new things, and it has helped him to remain a force in the sport. It might seem strange to the tennis youth, but the volley can be a weapon, whether it follows a serve, a 'Sneak Attack by Roger', or a more conventional approach shot. Federer can serve-and-volley. He can also return-and-volley. And off a regular rally-ball, he can charge-forward-and-volley.

●

Boris Becker, himself a superb volleyer, whether airborne or with his feet on the ground, said he admired 'Roger's great touch at the net'. In the summer of 2003, when Roger Federer won his first Wimbledon, he was serve-and-volleying almost half the time, according to official I.B.M. tournament data. The previous year, when he lost in the first round, he had followed his serve into the net at a rate of eighty-one per cent. Charging into the net had been the style of tennis Federer had become accustomed to watching. Serve-and-volley was also the strategy his first proper coach, Peter Carter, had advocated he should adopt. That dash into the service box, so unnerving for some, was fine for Federer. Indeed, in his first years on Tour, he felt he had a greater chance of success when he was playing volleys rather than groundstrokes against the hard-core baseliners like Andre Agassi, David Nalbandian and Lleyton Hewitt.

Yet, as the years went by, Federer stopped taking so many balls out of the air. That serve-and-volleying percentage dipped to below twenty per cent at Wimbledon in 2004, fell further in 2005, and from 2006 to 2012 it was under ten per cent. There was a slight climb in 2013, the year he lost to Sergiy Stakhovsky, but only to a mite over ten per cent. There was only one player on court that day truly using serve-and-volley tactics and that was the Ukrainian. If Federer was not going to serve-and-volley on grass, then where on earth

▶ OVERLEAF
Federer plays
Novak Djokovic
in the 2015 US
Open final.

would he? This decline in attacking tennis had much to do with the slowing of the Wimbledon grass, or at least the perception of it. The head groundsman will tell you that the courts are no slower now than when the blend of grass was changed in the early 2000s; the players will suggest otherwise. Federer tended to adapt his game to how others were playing. Rather than throwing himself forward, he found comfort on the baseline, where he could 'stay back, serve, wait and then hit the big forehand'.

But then came the 2014 Championships, the first since the collaboration with Stefan Edberg began, and Federer's rate of serve-and-volleying doubled from the summer before to twenty-two per cent. Such an approach would take him into his first Grand Slam final for two years. In the championship match, where he extended Novak Djokovic to five sets, Federer took forty-four points at the net. Added together, they would have been enough to win him eleven games, or almost two sets. 'Roger was playing some incredible volleys,' Djokovic said. Others would say it was the Roger of old. It was not quite. But it was about halfway there. It was a considerable break from the recent past, and one brought about by Edberg. That summer Federer wore a T-shirt with 'Betterer' printed across the chest, and in the closing weeks of the year he would challenge Djokovic's status as the number one. Such a revival would not have been possible without Edberg's soft, wise, persistent words of encouragement, which restored Federer's faith in moving to the net and hitting volleys.

▼ Federer got a thrill from hiring his idol.

PERCENTAGE OF RALLIES
WON BY SHOTS

0-4
56%

5-8
55%

9+
51%

Right at the close of the season, at the Davis Cup final in Lille, came what Federer described as 'a beautiful weekend of tennis', under the captaincy of Severin Lüthi. He defeated France's Richard Gasquet to give Switzerland the trophy for the first time. It was quite some way for Federer to end his first year with Edberg, even though the Swede was not present at courtside in Lille.

A thoughtful and intelligent man, Edberg was never going to urge Federer to serve-and-volley with the same regularity and abandon with which he had attacked the net in his day. The sport had moved on since then. All-out attack would be foolish. What Edberg was proposing was that Federer ventured forward much more than he had been.

Edberg was not the first of Federer's coaches to do important work on his volleys. Peter Lundgren once told the Swiss journalist René Stauffer how Federer 'hated volleys'. It was a surprising comment given how Federer's idols, and Peter Carter, played the game. 'Roger played as if sharks were lurking at the net in the service box,' Lundgren said. 'We drove off the sharks by training a lot.' Tony Roche also assisted Federer with his net game. But Edberg's intervention was huge. Whatever Edberg said in his private conversations with Federer, it worked. The Swiss disclosed: 'Maybe Stefan reinforced the concept that it's possible, that I can actually do it.' Confidence is paramount for someone who serves and volleys, much more than for a player who stays on the baseline. When balls start whizzing past you, are you suddenly going to retreat to the baseline on every point? As Federer has noted, it is easy to serve-and-volley at 40–love, but can you do it at 15–30? 'You have to be able to see the overall picture and to see that it's worth it,' he said.

Federer and Edberg quickly found they could communicate easily, and sometimes, when no one was speaking, that took the form of comfortable silences. As a player Edberg had not sought out the bright lights or regarded himself as a superstar. When he was living in London he was happy to travel by Tube. As a coach he was also happy to keep it low-key. In this alliance of the two gentlemen of the Tour, the glory would all be the player's, which perhaps was not true of the contemporaneous partnerships between Ivan Lendl and Andy Murray or Becker and Djokovic.

Take Edberg's honesty when discussing his role in the unveiling of 'Sneak Attack By Roger' at the tournament in Cincinnati, which the Swede had not attended. Rather than claiming any credit, Edberg disclosed how the first he had known of S.A.B.R. had been when he had seen it on television. In fact, it

◀ The shorter the rally, the more likely Federer is to win it. This is the data from the 2015 Wimbledon Championships.

IN THIS ALLIANCE OF THE TWO GENTLEMEN OF THE TOUR, THE GLORY WOULD ALL BE THE PLAYER'S, WHICH PERHAPS WAS NOT TRUE OF THE CONTEMPORANEOUS PARTNERSHIPS BETWEEN IVAN LENDL AND ANDY MURRAY OR BECKER AND DJOKOVIC.

had been Lüthi who was instrumental in the use of the S.A.B.R., which involved playing half-volley returns when just short of the service-line and then rushing in towards the net. Federer enjoyed hitting the new shot in practice, but it was Lüthi who urged him to take it from training to competition, telling Federer not to be afraid of using S.A.B.R. 'in the big moments'.

It would be a mistake, though, to reduce Edberg's contribution merely to his success at getting Federer to the net. For instance, he tweaked Federer's approach to training between tournaments. Previously, Federer would often not play points during practice weeks, only doing so in the days before an event. But Edberg convinced Federer that he should always play points in practice, regardless of when he was next in competition, so he maintained his rhythm. Still, it was when persuading Federer to play more volleys that he earned his salary and any bonuses. At the 2015 Wimbledon Championships, when Federer finished runner-up to Djokovic for the second successive summer, he served-and-volleyed sixteen per cent of the time. While this was around six per cent lower than the previous year's tournament, it was still considerably more than the overall average for all players of ten per cent, and far higher than Djokovic's two per cent.

More than any other member of the Big Four, Federer's inclination has always been to attack. Being the aggressor in the rally sat comfortably with his general approach to tennis. As a teenager, and then in his twenties, Federer had always aimed to finish off points as quickly as possible, whether from the back of the court or from an advanced position at the net. Now, in his thirties, there was even more reason for Federer to take the initiative and shorten the rallies. That way he could avoid the baseline grind. True, he might be passed or lobbed, or out-manoeuvred in some other way, but at least he would not be playing fetch along the baseline. Federer would be playing tennis on his terms.

●

The story of how Roger Federer came to switch to a larger racket is one littered with more than a hundred prototypes. Maybe even double that number, as according to some technicians at Wilson, the Chicago-based company who supply Federer's rackets, there were more than 250 different versions of the new frame under development. 'To Roger's credit, he was able to make the adjustment to a new racket,' said Nate Ferguson, whose company cares for Federer's rackets. 'I remember working for a year and a half trying to develop a racket with Pete Sampras and he just kept on wanting the new racket to play exactly like his old racket. Roger, though, enjoyed the process of testing different rackets and working with Wilson to find a racket that would improve his game and give him easier power. Pete had all the power in the world and he was all about controlling the power with his racket. Roger realised he needed to add power to keep up with the speed of today's tennis.'

In addition to hiring Stefan Edberg, and an improvement in his troublesome back, an enlarged racket was fundamental to Federer's approach. For any tennis player, switching from one 'bat' to another is no small matter. Federer's decision would be one of the most critical of his career, and certainly not one he would make without an extended period of testing, tinkering,

▼ Federer delights the crowd by playing a shot through his legs.

WINNING RECORD

Federer's winning percentage by surfaces
(correct up to end of 2017)

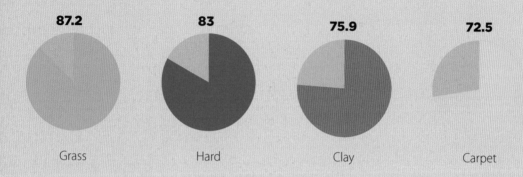

| **87.2** | **83** | **75.9** | **72.5** |
| Grass | Hard | Clay | Carpet |

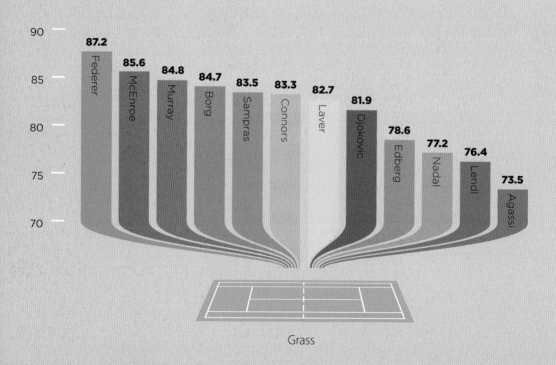

Grass

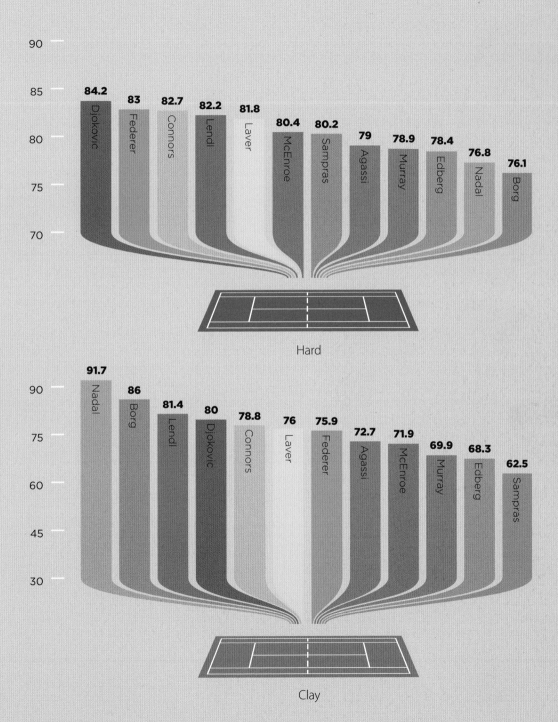

Hard

Clay

chin-scratching and further experimentation. After all, Federer had won seventeen Grand Slams with a racket that was unique to him: with a head size of only ninety square inches, it was the smallest on the Tour. 'Changing rackets is a tricky thing, a mental thing,' Federer has said. When he was younger Federer had always felt he should be using a smaller racket, his thinking influenced by his adoration of Pete Sampras and Stefan Edberg, both of whom had played with eighty-five-square-inch rackets. He had used a racket of that size before making the change to ninety square inches. For the best part of a decade he did not go any bigger than that. His rivals were enlarging their rackets, to give them more power and a bigger sweet-spot, but Federer kept it old school. It was not as if he had not been thinking about it, though. He was not deaf to the science or the advances in technology. For a while, some had been urging Federer to experiment with a larger frame, which would be more forgiving at those moments when the ball did not connect with the middle of the strings. For all his talent Federer has always shanked more shots than his rivals. Would a larger racket not add some more power to his game, as well as being more forgiving? Sampras, who stuck with that eighty-five-square-inch racket throughout his career, but changed to a large frame to play exhibition matches in retirement, has since expressed regret that he did not do so in his heyday.

It was during the opening weeks of the 2013 season that Federer informed Wilson that he was interested in moving to a frame larger than his Pro Staff. After the Australian Open some of the company's technicians flew to Switzerland for detailed testing with a bunch of different prototypes with larger heads. But those were early days and Federer would switch back to his ninety-square-inch frame for the summer. Still, after the disappointment of the defeat by Sergiy Stakhovsky at Wimbledon, he let it be known he was more committed to change. It was then that the bulk of the testing, rejecting and refining took place. In the racket laboratory everything was looked at, questioned, challenged and then remodelled. The variations included the size of the head, the stiffness of the frame, the balance point of the racket, and how the racket was constructed. Wilson gave Federer blacked-out rackets to test in practice, and also to use in tournaments, because they did not want any colour schemes to have an effect on the player's feedback.

◀ Federer on the attack at the 2015 US Open.

DURING THE GOLDEN YEARS OF HIS TENNIS LIFE, WHEN HE WON SEVENTEEN GRAND SLAMS, FEDERER HAD USED A RACKET WITH A HEAD SIZE OF ONLY NINETY SQUARE INCHES, THE SMALLEST ON THE TOUR.

Federer made a permanent switch to a larger frame at the conclusion of his disappointing 2013. The racket would become known as the Wilson Pro Staff RF97 Autograph, with the number a reference to its square inches. In the end he had settled on an increase of seven square inches, or around eight per cent, on what he had been using before. But even with that sizeable jump, Federer's racket was still the smallest of those used by the Big Four. Novak Djokovic and Rafa Nadal were both believed to be using a racket of one hundred square inches, while Andy Murray's frame was ninety-eight square inches. Any weekend hacker who picked up Federer's old racket would not have found it easy to play with. Neither was the new frame particularly accessible to amateurs with its weight of 340 grams, around forty grams heavier than a regular custom frame.

Federer's decision to switch rackets should not be viewed as a sign of weakness. Nor was it a panicky move. Together with the technicians he built on what had gone before. It was a bold move, but it was also a smart, calculated and eminently sensible one. His surge in form in 2014 underlines that. Every part of Federer's game was altered by the change. He believes that the new racket produced an increase in power and also gave him an improvement in his first-serve percentage. Ferguson agrees. 'Roger has a bigger serve now, for sure. The racket has meant it's easier for him to hit aces.' The extra power in the racket has enabled Federer to shorten the backswing for both his forehand and backhand. More compact strokes mean he can play higher up the court, often on or inside the baseline, so he can reach the net quicker. Those extra square inches, Rod Laver said, have meant Federer is attacking more with his backhand. 'Roger now has more speed with his backhand, especially when hitting down the line,' Laver explained. 'Since moving to that new racket he has been hitting the ball harder and being more aggressive.'

●

Novak Djokovic's voice spiked just a little, but enough to reveal that the subject of conversation was making him emotional. He was talking about the day he defeated Roger Federer in the 2014 Wimbledon final by winning a

FEDERER'S MOST SUCCESSFUL COACH? HIMSELF

Severin Lüthi has also been part of Federer's team for more than 10 years

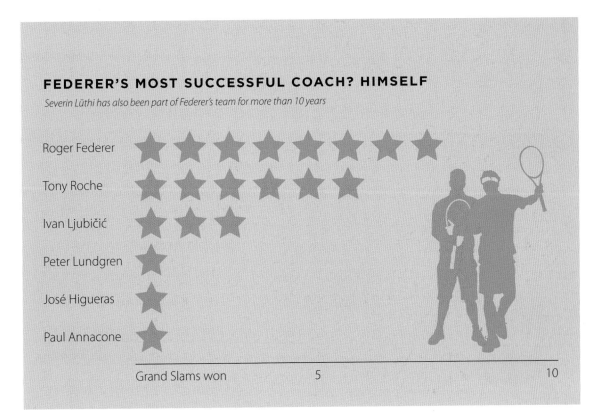

	Grand Slams won	5	10
Roger Federer	★★★★★★★★★		
Tony Roche	★★★★★★★		
Ivan Ljubičić	★★★		
Peter Lundgren	★		
José Higueras	★		
Paul Annacone	★		

five-setter of the rarest quality and tension. 'It was a dream scenario for me to win Wimbledon by beating one of the best players in the history of the game, the guy who has a record number of Wimbledon titles, and on his own court, the court that he has dominated for so many years. And then to win a marathon match, I couldn't have scripted that any better. On the court I felt the flow of emotions coming out,' Djokovic said. 'Those are the moments you work for on a daily basis. You have this vision, this dream, in your head that you want to be on Centre Court at Wimbledon, fighting against one of your biggest rivals for the title. And then you envisage yourself winning that title. So when you actually do that, and experience all those feelings, it's just magical.'

It is a curious part of the Federer story, considering the feats he accomplished at the All England Club, that arguably the two greatest matches he has played there are defeats. The first one to Rafa Nadal in the 2008 final, and then six summers later to Djokovic. Maybe that is a sign of Federer's excellence, that it takes something special for an opponent to bring him down. After saving a match-point in the fourth set against Djokovic, he put himself just one set away from winning Wimbledon for the eighth time. With Djokovic serving at 4–4, 15–all in the fifth set, Federer had what appeared to

▶ Federer uses aggressive tactics against Djokovic in the 2015 US Open final.

be a fairly straightforward smash, only to drag the ball down into the net. It is at those moments that television commentators like to say that Federer could play that shot one hundred times, and probably make ninety-nine of them. How would Djokovic have coped with being 15–30 down? As it was Djokovic would hold serve to 15, and then break Federer in the next game.

Had Federer prevailed, that match may well have superseded the 2008 Wimbledon final on the unofficial list of the greatest tennis matches in history. 'For one of the guys involved in a match like that – and on this occasion it was Roger – it's going to be painful to speak about, so I wouldn't try to have a conversation with Roger,' Djokovic said. 'For the winner, when you have a dream match like that, it's kind of nice to remind yourself about it, that you went through that experience. You don't really talk about it, but both guys involved in a match like that, we both know that they are the moments that are going to stay in your heads for a long time.'

The following year Federer reached another Wimbledon final thanks to his brilliant serving performance against Andy Murray in the semi-final. In the immediate aftermath Federer's father, Robert, said his son was far from past it. 'This is proof that Roger is still around and he can still play good tennis. Is it more satisfying that Roger has reached a Wimbledon final at the age of thirty-three, and not long before he turns thirty-four? That's a good question. Roger isn't as old as some people think he is, and were writing two years ago [when he lost in the second round].' For the second summer in succession at Wimbledon, Djokovic, and Djokovic alone, prevented Federer from adding to his Grand Slam tally. Djokovic said he believed this golden generation – Rafa Nadal, Andy Murray and himself – had brought out the best in Federer. At the same time Federer and others had brought out the best in Djokovic. As some would have it, it is Federer who has helped create this monster. And a defensive monster at that. No one attacks quite like Federer, and no one repels and defends others' attacking tennis as Djokovic can.

▶ Federer plays Djokovic in the 2015 Wimbledon final.

▶▶
OVERLEAF
Federer and Djokovic do a lap of Centre Court after the 2015 Wimbledon final.

Having fun with his new toy, his 'Sneak Attack By Roger', Federer reached the final of the 2015 US Open for the loss of just fifty-two games. Only once before had he dropped so few games during the first six rounds of a Grand Slam, and that had been almost a decade earlier when he conceded the same number on the way to the final of the 2006 Wimbledon Championships. Unfortunately for Federer, though he had beaten Djokovic in hot, fast conditions in Cincinnati just a few weeks earlier, it was not to be in the

YOU COULD NOT MEET A MORE THOUGHTFUL AND INTELLIGENT SOUL IN TENNIS THAN IVAN LJUBIČIĆ. PERHAPS THAT APPROACH TO LIFE CAN BE TRACED TO HIS BACKGROUND AS A REFUGEE AMID THE HORRORS OF THE BALKAN WAR.

rain-delayed final in New York. For the third time in just over a year Djokovic had spiked the romantic story of Federer winning his eighteenth slam. Federer created plenty of break-point opportunities, twenty-three in all, but converted just four of them.

That run in New York City would be Federer's last Grand Slam with his 'childhood idol' as his sidekick. Federer disclosed just before Christmas 2015 that his association with Edberg had ended after two happy years together, twice as long as originally anticipated. Unlike the great majority of partnerships on the men's circuit, this collaboration did not finish with the coach being fired, cast aside like an old, unwashed sweat-band. Instead, here was the rare sight of both parties staying dignified and with each still speaking warmly of the other. 'They had a really successful run together, with Roger reaching three Grand Slam finals, and in all three of those Roger ran into a guy, Novak Djokovic, who was playing some phenomenal tennis,' Paul Annacone said.

So, Federer turned to Ivan Ljubičić for his coaching needs. In his day, Ljubičić's game-style was fundamentally as a baseline basher, quite different to Edberg. But that is not to say that Ljubičić's appointment would in any way wipe out what Federer and Edberg had accomplished together. Far from it. Federer was clear that Edberg had 'taught me so much, and his influence on my game will remain'. While Edberg would no longer be travelling the world with Federer, he would, in the words of the Swiss, 'always be a part of my team'.

●

For the first time, Roger Federer had hired a coach who had once been an opponent and frequent practice partner on the ATP World Tour. Sixteen times Federer and Ivan Ljubičić had met – with the Swiss victorious on thirteen occasions – and they had trained together dozens of times over the years.

If Federer's partnership with Stefan Edberg was founded on the Swiss looking up to the Swede, the next collaboration was based on something arguably even more meaningful: friendship. While Ljubičić did not have Edberg's standing in the sport, he had much going for him, not least that he had a close understanding and appreciation of the modern game, and in particular of Federer's tennis. Just two years older than Federer, Ljubičić had peaked at number three in the rankings, and although he did not appear in a Grand Slam final, he did venture as far as the semi-finals of the French Open one year, and also propelled Croatia to success in the Davis Cup. Since his retirement in 2012, he had maintained his connection with the sport through a number of roles, including television commentary, managing Tomáš Berdych and coaching Milos Raonic. While Ljubičić was known for the pop on his serve, perhaps his most pertinent expertise here was knowing how to attack with a single-handed backhand.

At six feet four inches tall, Ljubičić is an imposing figure. But despite his height and the might of his serve and groundstrokes, you could not meet a more thoughtful and intelligent soul in tennis. Perhaps that approach to life can be traced to his background as a refugee amid the horrors of the Balkan War. Ljubičić's family were living in Banja Luka, an area that was dominated by Serbians, now part of Bosnia and Herzegovina, when they realised that 'people were disappearing': they made their escape on a cargo plane. From there, they travelled by bus around Hungary and Slovenia before arriving at a refugee camp in Croatia. For Ljubičić to have made it to the ATP World Tour was remarkable in itself, but during his playing days he was a highly influential figure. As well as serving on the ATP Player Council, he was also on the ATP Board of Directors, which was the first time in almost twenty years that an active player had been at that level of the organisation.

Federer is not alone in tennis in regarding Ljubičić as 'very bright' and 'a natural leader', qualities which would prove useful when he came to coach Federer. Their player-coach relationship did not have an ideal start, as it was after their first Grand Slam together – the 2016 Australian Open, where Federer lost in the semi-finals – that the Swiss damaged his knee and underwent the first operation of his career. Federer's semi-final defeat at Wimbledon that year was to Ljubičić's old employer, Raonic. With Federer not playing again that season, Ljubičić was barely able to shape and influence his friend's tennis in a way he might have hoped.

However, in contrast, 2017 would turn out to be a remarkable year. That had quite a lot to do with Severin Lüthi's influence, but also the work that Ljubičić did to refresh and reinvigorate Federer's single-handed backhand.

9
THE RED ENVELOPE

OTHERS MIGHT CALL ROGER FEDERER'S MOST DEVOTED SUPPORTERS THE FED-HEADS OR THE FEDERER-PHILES, BUT THEY DO NOT HAVE A NAME FOR THEMSELVES. WHAT THEY DO HAVE A NAME FOR, THOUGH, ARE THE GOOD-LUCK MESSAGES THEY HAND-DELIVER TO FEDERER AT EVERY TOURNAMENT: THE RED ENVELOPE

The morning after the 2015 men's singles final at the All England Club, an image of a tennis player in his Wimbledon whites dominated the front page of one British newspaper. It was not the champion, Novak Djokovic, who had put himself level with his coach Boris Becker, as well as John McEnroe, by winning a third title on Centre Court. That photograph, big, striking and above the fold, was of the runner-up, Roger Federer. How could Djokovic possibly compete with Federer's tale of 'Heartbreak for Wimbledon's Adopted Son'?

It was certainly not the first time, nor will it be the last, that another tennis player had been denied their moment, their cover, their close-up, because of the public's adoration for Federer. That newspaper's editor was only giving the public what they wanted. Djokovic's treatment by the British media was benign compared to how some of the New York tennis public roughed him up a couple of months later in the US Open final when he again played Federer. Spectators inside the Arthur Ashe Stadium applauded Djokovic's errors, including faults on his first serve. And every now and then a few boos would come rolling down from the stands. This was adoration for Federer tipping over into hostility for his opponent, seemingly fuelled by the beer that had been consumed while the crowd waited for the rain to clear. Apart from Becker, Djokovic's wife, Jelena, and Hollywood actor Gerard Butler, this was essentially the Serbian against New York. To cope, Djokovic tried to fool himself into thinking the crowd was on his side: 'They would scream "Roger" and I would imagine they were screaming "Novak".' The other two members of the Big Four have faced similar antipathy in their matches against Federer. For all that Rafa Nadal has achieved on the clay of Roland Garros, and

▶ Federer's Wimbledon outfits are the closest that tennis has come to haute couture.

no one has won more titles at any one Grand Slam, many Parisians make no secret of their preference for Federer. Then there was the time Andy Murray turned up at the 2012 season-ending tournament in the east of London, for what was his first event in Britain since victory at the US Open. Perhaps Murray, who had just become the first British man to win a major since the 1930s, would have expected the London crowd to have been heavily in his favour. As it turned out, it was very much a pro-Federer gallery. It might almost have been Basel's St. Jakobshalle.

●

Others might call Roger Federer's most devoted supporters the Fed-Heads or the Federer-philes, but they do not have a name for themselves. What they do have a name for, though, are the good-luck messages they hand-deliver to Federer at every tournament: The Red Envelope. For all the enthusiasm with which Federer embraces social media – he used the power that comes from having millions of Twitter followers to successfully lobby for the creation of a popcorn emoji – it is somehow refreshing to know that his fanbase use a method of communication that pre-dates Twitter and Facebook. These missives reveal an adoration that goes beyond wearing an 'R.F.' baseball cap, 'R.F.' T-shirt or even 'R.F.' earrings. Here is a love which seems to be baked into the soul. To call it an obsession would be to risk under-selling the strength of feeling.

It was in 2003, the year Federer won his first major, that The Red Envelope came into being. One of his fans had developed the idea of collecting letters and messages of encouragement which would then be presented to him at pre-tournament practice. Federer likes the written or printed word. As an aspiring young player he would inform a former coach, Madeleine Bärlocher, that he had won a title by sending a telegram to Basel. At first, it was only at the Grand Slams that the fans handed Federer the envelope, sealed with an official sticker, but now they do it at almost every tournament he plays. 'Roger lets you in and lets you care about him. I feel very protective of him, as a big sister would,' one of Federer's most committed fans, Colleen Taylor, explained. 'I usually contribute a short message for every tournament. I have been The Red Envelope courier twice. It's a great experience because Roger knows all about the tradition and he knows to be on the look-out for us. At the practice courts the courier can usually get Roger's attention by holding up The Red Envelope and then Roger makes sure to approach that person to receive it.'

Spotting the contributors is not difficult as many of them will be collected around the red-and-white banner courtside requesting: 'Shh. Quiet. Genius at Work.' The banner was Taylor's idea. In the spring of 2006 she was going to the Miami tournament with her friends Judith and Christina for what she called a first 'live sighting' of Federer. The banner commemorates that trip. 'Roger had just won Indian Wells, and there was an article written about that victory where the author used those great phrases and we chose to use them, too.' For the best part of a decade the banner has been wherever Federer has been. 'We held the banner up at Roger's first match at the Miami tournament and the Associated Press took a picture. After the tournament Judith didn't want to just throw the banner away, so she posted a message on RogerFederer.com and asked if anyone wanted to take it to another tournament. The legend was born,' said Taylor, who lives in Texas and works in I.T. 'In addition to holding it up, fans also sign it. It started gaining notoriety with fans and Roger started recognising it.'

No other player has generated this much love. Not even Bjorn Borg when

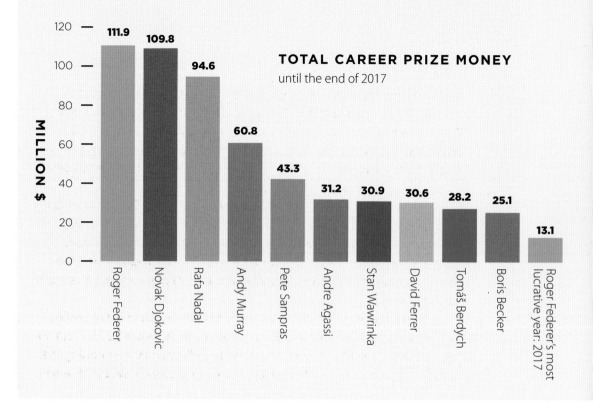

TOTAL CAREER PRIZE MONEY
until the end of 2017

MILLION $

- Roger Federer — 111.9
- Novak Djokovic — 109.8
- Rafa Nadal — 94.6
- Andy Murray — 60.8
- Pete Sampras — 43.3
- Andre Agassi — 31.2
- Stan Wawrinka — 30.9
- David Ferrer — 30.6
- Tomáš Berdych — 28.2
- Boris Becker — 25.1
- Roger Federer's most lucrative year: 2017 — 13.1

he was the Viking god of the Wimbledon lawns, and the All England Club secretary would write to the headmistresses of the local girls' schools asking them to control their pupils. It was while visiting Brazil, during a mini off-season exhibition tour in South America, that Federer experienced hysteria of the sort that even he found bewildering. 'I met more fans who collapsed in tears than elsewhere. It was amazing how many were shaking. I had to practically take them in my arms and say, "It's OK, it's OK"'. And that was in a country where Federer had never played before. In New York, a city accustomed to having Federer around in late summer, they do not behave that differently. Such was the crush of people who wanted his autograph during one US Open, he was immediately concerned when he spotted a six-year-old boy and had security staff scoop up the child and put him down on the court. Even when Federer is not around he can still cause mayhem: in Shanghai a Federer impersonator – and not even a very good one – was surrounded as he walked the city's streets. Some of Federer's most committed and excitable supporters are inside the tennis V.I.P. tent, not outside peering in. Chris Evert's emotional control as a player was such that she was known as the

Ice Queen. But these days, as a commentator, she finds herself brought to tears by Federer's tennis. 'Why do I love Roger? I don't know, I just love him. There is something about Roger which just tugs at the heartstrings. I don't know what it is exactly, but he just gets to me. I've been in this game for more than forty years now, and there has never been a player who has made me as emotional as Roger has, not even close.'

It is not hard to appreciate why Federer keeps on winning the award for being the most adored player on Tour, as voted for by the fans. His victory in 2017 marked fifteen unbroken years of success in that popularity contest. 'Borg was kind of loved, but not loved like this,' said Mats Wilander. 'This has never happened before in tennis, and I don't think it's ever happened before in any other sport.'

It is sometimes said by others that the only place Federer is not treated like a superstar is in Switzerland, the only nation where he can lead something approaching a quiet life between tournaments. 'All around the world, Roger is almost like a holy cow, but that's not the case in Switzerland, people are a bit

▼ Federer is adored around the world.

more reserved,' observed someone close to the Federer camp. Certainly, Martina Hingis has remarked that Swiss tennis fans do not press off-duty tennis players for autographs in the same way that, say, Americans do. And it is true Federer needed to win three Grand Slams before the Old Boys Tennis Club put a portrait of him on the wall of the clubhouse, or before they renamed one of the courts in his honour. Even so, you wonder whether that point has been overstated. Federer's brilliance cuts through a lot of that traditional Swiss reserve. After all, this is the man who received votes in a Swiss election in which he was not even a candidate, with fans adding his name to the ballot papers. And it was when Federer travelled to the alpine tournament in Gstaad in Switzerland after winning his maiden Wimbledon title that he first experienced what fame really felt like. Suddenly everyone wanted a piece of him, whether he was on court, in the hotel lobby, or walking around the resort town. With every additional Grand Slam triumph, Federer's celebrity grew. While still in his mid-twenties he became the first living Swiss to be depicted on a stamp. 'I'm proud to be a symbol of Switzerland,' Federer has said, 'like the army knife or the mountains.'

●

'Everything Roger does on a tennis court – even when the ball isn't in play, and he's flicking it to a ball-kid – is cool,' Mats Wilander said as he tried to explain the global adoration for Federer. Clearly, there is more to this than mere numbers and records. 'His passion for tennis is so genuine. But, more than anything, it's his technique. He plays tennis the way you would like to see tennis played, but with a modern twist. It's so effortless. It looks as though he's floating. There is also the way he behaves on and off the court, but I would say that his technique is the most important reason that he is so widely loved around the world.' That class and technique makes his nationality almost irrelevant. The tennis galleries have never been the most partisan of sports fans. They are far less interested in his passport than in how he moves and hits the ball. The fact that he is not one of those modern-day grunters also matters.

Federer's 'perfect hair' helps, Wilander said, as do his looks and maybe even the way he walks between points. He has been included in *People* magazine's 'Sexiest Man Alive' issue in the 'International men of sexiness' section. In Pete Sampras's analysis, though, the core of Federer's appeal is his

Roger-Federer-Allee

Tennis-Weltstar
Rekordsieger GERRY WEBER OPEN

▲ A street in Halle in Germany, which hosts a grass-court tournament, is named after Federer.

humility. That is a theory strengthened in a study by the Reputation Institute which found that Federer was the second most trusted and respected figure in the world, behind only Nelson Mandela. Around 50,000 people, from twenty-five countries, were interviewed a few years before Mandela passed away, with the Pope, Barack Obama and the Queen trailing Federer. 'What makes Roger so popular and so endearing is that he doesn't go around saying he's a record-breaker. Instead he is humble and just goes out and plays,' Sampras said. 'I don't think Roger realises how good he is, and what a great champion he is. He never thinks he's better than you. That's what makes him so appealing. I just like what Roger is about, how he carries himself and how he goes about things, and a lot of other people like the same things.'

Very occasionally the adulation can unsettle Federer. On that off-season trip to South America in 2012, the one that might be termed 'The Hysteria Tour', he tried to convey calmness as his weeping fans collapsed and genuflected before him. But, despite appearances, he was not calm inside. Adoration on this scale can take some getting used to. As Federer once disclosed: 'I have to constantly remind myself where I come from and to tell myself who I am.' He is able to do that, he told the Zurich newspaper *Tages-*

1,000 VICTORIES

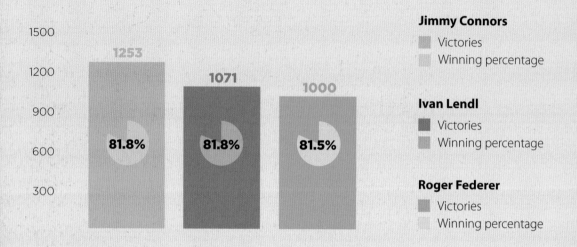

1500
1200
900
600
300

1253

81.8%

1071

81.8%

1000

81.5%

Jimmy Connors
- Victories
- Winning percentage

Ivan Lendl
- Victories
- Winning percentage

Roger Federer
- Victories
- Winning percentage

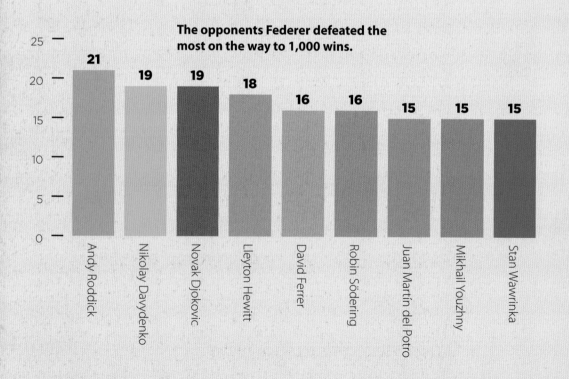

The opponents Federer defeated the most on the way to 1,000 wins.

25
20
15
10
5
0

Andy Roddick	Nikolay Davydenko	Novak Djokovic	Lleyton Hewitt	David Ferrer	Robin Söderling	Juan Martín del Potro	Mikhail Youzhny	Stan Wawrinka
21	19	19	18	16	16	15	15	15

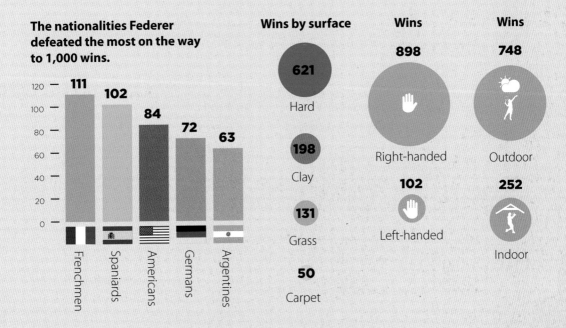

The nationalities Federer defeated the most on the way to 1,000 wins.

Frenchmen	111
Spaniards	102
Americans	84
Germans	72
Argentines	63

Wins by surface

621 Hard
198 Clay
131 Grass
50 Carpet

Wins

898 Right-handed
102 Left-handed

Wins

748 Outdoor
252 Indoor

Milestone victories

1	Guillaume Raoux (France) in the first round in Toulouse in 1998.
100	Julien Boutter (France) in the semi-finals in Basel in 2001.
200	Mikhail Youzhny (Russia) in the semi-finals in Halle in 2003.
300	Lleyton Hewitt (Australia) in the US Open final in 2004.
400	Tommy Haas (Germany) in the fourth round of the Australian Open in 2006.
500	David Ferrer (Spain) in the quarter-finals in Monte Carlo in 2007.
600	Thiago Alves (Brazil) in the second round of the US Open in 2008.
700	Julien Reister (Germany) in the third round of the French Open in 2010.
800	Juan Monaco (Argentina) in the quarter-finals of the Paris Indoors in 2011.
900	Gilles Simon (France) in the fourth round of the French Open in 2013.
1000	Milos Raonic (Canada) in the final in Brisbane in 2015.

Anzeiger, by returning to a 'normal life'. That sense of normality is enhanced by the knowledge that what happens in his personal life will remain private. Federer's circle does not 'leak'. We know that to be true because the thirty or so guests who attended Federer and Mirka's wedding did not let slip when it was taking place. The first the media and the public knew of the wedding was when Federer announced it. The same was true when Mirka gave birth to their twin girls. It had generally been thought that she was pregnant with just one child.

Equilibrium restored, Federer then feels able to 'dip back into the incredible life I have'. Fame did not sit comfortably with some past champions, such as Sampras, but as a young man Federer had always felt he wanted celebrity. It was a desire no doubt intensified during the early days on Tour when fans would ask him if he was Tommy Haas or Carlos Moyá. While some encounters with his public can be a little unnerving, Federer continues to enjoy being an icon. As he said once: 'I like being the star. I love being the magnet of people's attention.' It is just as well that he does, otherwise his life would be intolerable. Indeed, Federer has become completely accustomed to his elevated status. He is forever scheduled to be on centre stage, apart from those rare times at the Grand Slams when he plays on the second largest stadium, such as Court Suzanne Lenglen at Roland Garros. Not that Federer minds, but he does not think he would be able to maintain the same motivation if he was playing on an outside court in front of a smattering of spectators.

●

Naturally, there has been a transformation in the man from his early days on the Tour as a rough-around-the-edges teenager who once returned from a junior tournament in America with a 250-dollar head of bleached blond hair. Federer's parents were upset, his coaches and friends amused. 'Roger came to the club wearing a hat and at first he refused to take it off,' a coach at the Old Boys Tennis Club said. 'He was embarrassed. But he won't ever be allowed to forget about that hairstyle as there are photos of it in the club.' A few years later Federer would wear his hair shoulder-length, in keeping with his liking for rock music. Together with his then coach Peter Lundgren, whose hair was in the same style, the pair resembled a couple of roadies. The polish, the comportment and the perfect, preppy hair? They would come later. Federer's other interests included, for a while, the Backstreet Boys pop group, and American wrestling, which he appreciated for the showmanship and theatre, in particular the wrestlers The Undertaker and The Rock. Many of today's tennis youth spend their down-time on the PlayStation, and Federer was no different in his younger days, with a James Bond game a particular favourite. Sometimes Federer would involve Lundgren in these games, and Lundgren has recalled how, on the rare occasions he won, Federer might fling the console across the hotel room. 'Don't worry,' Federer would say. 'I'll buy another one.' Who could have imagined then, when he was a long-haired gamer, that Federer's future friends would include the heir to the British throne and his consort, William and Kate, the Duke and Duchess of Cambridge? Or that GQ magazine would judge him to be the most stylish man of 2016, and he would attend the Met Ball in New York in 2017 wearing a flamboyant Gucci jacket with a cobra depicted in crystals on the back?

The first time Federer met Anna Wintour, the editor-in-chief of American *Vogue* and the inspiration for the book and film *The Devil Wears Prada*, he did not know who she was. So deeply did Federer care for fashion at that time that it is said he only had two pairs of jeans in his wardrobe. After that first encounter, at the 2002 US Open, Wintour would become arguably Federer's biggest 'celebrity' admirer, though at one stage rock star Gavin Rossdale, tennis player Chris Evert and golfer Tiger Woods would have run her close. At many of the most important moments in Federer's tennis life, Wintour has been there, whether as a guest in his box or in the V.I.P. seats behind the baseline. She has even been known to leave fashion shows early to watch his matches on television. Over the years Wintour has become a close friend as well as an unofficial adviser. One year she hosted a party for him at a restaurant in Manhattan. According to Wintour, she has escorted Federer to shows and the Swiss has come to love the 'creativity, humour and personality of fashion'. Certainly, he does not now want to be photographed again and again wearing 'the same blue jumper'. 'I spend a lot of money on clothes – I see them as an investment,' Federer said.

For years, one of the rituals of summer was the anticipation of Federer's Wimbledon outfit, and then the critique that followed. This is about the closest that men's tennis has ever come to haute couture. Some saw Wintour's influence in Federer's high fashion moments, though it would appear from her

▲ Federer at a fashion show with his friend Anna Wintour, the editor-in-chief of American *Vogue*.

comments to the *New Yorker* magazine that she advised him to tone down some of his gold-flecked and gold-trimmed outfits: 'Roger does like a bit of flash.' Those outfits all had to be cleared in advance by the All England Club to ensure they adhered to the almost-all-white rule. Despite these restrictions, or perhaps because of them, Federer's clothing suppliers Nike have been hugely creative, starting in 2006 with the retro blazer and the personal crest on the breast pocket. The following summer it was a blazer and pair of flannel trousers, which invoked comparisons with the glitter of F. Scott Fitzgerald's *The Great Gatsby*. In all the excitement that followed the victory over Nadal with which he became the first man to win five successive Wimbledon titles since Borg, Federer put his trousers on back-to-front for the prize-giving ceremony. Inevitably, there was criticism of Federer for what he wore, but there was a sense that the fashion police were taking it too seriously. To make his entrance in 2008 he wore a five-button herringbone cardigan over his shirt. In 2009 came what was described as his 'angel-soldier look' – a white, military-style suit, accessorised with a waistcoat and a gold lamé and white bag. Federer did not want people to think he was 'trying to show off' and this was 'too much bling bling'. The point of the gold was to have a connection between the outfit and the trophy. In subsequent years, though, Federer's Wimbledon garb has become a little more subdued. He did say, however, that he thought the rules were 'ridiculously strict', a comment perhaps influenced by the time he was asked to change his orange-soled shoes.

It was not just at Wimbledon that Federer's clothes attracted comment. One year at the US Open he was called Darth Federer because of his all-black get-up during the night sessions. The idea was that he looked as though he was wearing something approaching a tuxedo under the lights of the Arthur Ashe Stadium. Such is Federer's interest in tennis fashion that he keeps three of every outfit, which must take up a lot of wardrobe space since Nike change his look between ten and a dozen times every season.

Stylistically, nothing is quite so important to the Federer brand than the R.F. monogram that has come to adorn almost everything he wears. The first Federer logo was based upon his signature and used to market his own fragrance. While the perfume has not survived, the idea of having a logo has. The next stage was the personal crest, or coat of arms, that he introduced in London in 2006. It incorporated a Swiss cross, a tuft of grass, his Leo star sign, the 'F' from his surname, and three rackets representing the three Wimbledon titles he had won to that point. The R.F. monogram would follow, as would the caps, T-shirts and all sorts of other branded merchandise. Football supporters have long been able to show their allegiance in the stands with their clothes and headgear; Federer likes how his followers can do the same. Federer is very comfortable with his status. There is a spoof Twitter account, @PseudoFed, which affectionately mocks Federer for his supposed self-satisfaction. But just because Federer does not go in for false

▼ Federer poses in a Wimbledon outfit.

modesty does not make him arrogant.

One year, anyone walking up the hill from the All England Club to Wimbledon Village would have passed a church which displayed a banner reading: 'God made Roger Federer.' All this love for Federer, not just from the centre court congregations but from the clergy as well, can be profoundly upsetting for Federer's rivals, even if they try to fool themselves, as Novak Djokovic did during the 2015 US Open final. 'This is tricky, though I also don't think anyone has the right to even think they should be as a popular as Roger,' Mats Wilander said. 'And if you find yourself comparing yourself in popularity terms with Federer, then you should have gone into a different business. The problem is that crowds are always rooting for Federer, so if you beat him it feels as though you are going to spoil the party. And that sucks for a player. To have that every time you play against Federer, that's going to be tough for your spirits.'

Djokovic, greatly admired but not universally loved, has spoken of how difficult he found it to deal with the public's love for Federer. 'Roger is a legend of the court, and he has made history, and because of his success, and because of who he is on and off the court, he is often the crowd favourite. That is difficult for me. I won't lie, it's tough. At the beginning of my career it felt a bit strange. I was confused about how to get people on my side,' he told *The Times Magazine*. 'But you cannot blame the crowd. That's just the way it is.'

Like everyone else in the locker room, Djokovic does not blame Federer either. The players struggle to work themselves into a fury at how Federer has snaffled not just so many trophies, but so many fans' allegiances, too. Why, one of Federer's contemporaries on the Tour, John Isner, used to co-run a Facebook page: 'If tennis is a religion, Roger Federer is God.' One summer at Wimbledon Federer hit a lobbed tweener over Sam Querrey's head, and the American felt a compulsion to walk around the net and 'high-five Roger'. Thankfully he checked himself, as it would not have been appropriate. 'You want to beat Roger, but he's fun to watch, too,' Querrey said. 'It's a damn war out there,' Jimmy Connors once said of life on centre court. But that was in the wild days of the 1980s, and it is not how it has been during the Age of Federer. By comparison, this is a time of flowers-in-the-hair hippies and peaceniks.

One of the difficulties for Federer's rivals over the years, John McEnroe once suggested, is that the Swiss is so likeable that they have found it impossible to fuel themselves for competition with any bitterness or enmity.

'Federer is a classy guy and maybe that's the problem, that it's difficult to find anything wrong with him. I don't think there's a guy in the locker room who doesn't like Roger Federer. I don't think you could have said the same thing about me or Jimmy Connors or some of the other guys who have held the number one ranking in the past.' Wilander agreed: 'The problem for guys like Nadal and Murray and Djokovic is that it's not easy to find a reason to think that a match against Federer is a match worth getting angry about. Instead, they're thinking that Roger's a good guy and that he's got a cool game and that he has won everything in tennis.' Perhaps it is really true that this age of civility has prevented Federer's rivals from playing eyeballs-out tennis against him, and that good manners have ambushed ambition. But not everyone thinks like McEnroe or Connors, or needs to be fuelled with indignation as well as bananas and isotonic drinks. More likely, it has been Federer's tennis, rather than his pleasant nature, that has brought him success.

Coffee-table books do not tend to be controversial, but in a 2015 publication on his life at Wimbledon to mark thirty years since he won the tournament as a seventeen year old, Boris Becker suggested it was 'an open secret' that Federer and Becker's employer, Djokovic, 'don't particularly like each other'. He also wrote: 'The reason Roger is one of the highest-paid athletes of all time is because he's liked by everybody. But think about this – you cannot possibly be liked by everybody or you have no character. Now I'm not saying Roger has no character because he clearly has. What I'm saying is that it's just an impossible image to portray, so why try?'

This was surprising, especially as it did not come long after the German had described Federer as 'the greatest ambassador in the sport's history', and how he had carried tennis for years. Now, it is true Federer was not entirely happy with Djokovic's behaviour when the Serbian was new on the scene, when Djokovic was in the habit of doing impersonations of players. In Federer's words, he had not been 'crazy impressed' by Djokovic, who had been 'walking a tightrope'. But Djokovic had modified his behaviour and that tension had long since disappeared. Federer did once tell Djokovic's parents to 'be quiet, OK?' during a match at the Monte Carlo Country Club, but again that was a long time ago, and was not representative either of Federer's character or of his feelings towards Djokovic and his family.

Federer was taken aback by the assertions in Becker's book and said they were categorically untrue. 'Becker has no clue. He should know me well

▶ OVERLEAF
Federer and
Andre Agassi play
tennis on a
helipad as they
promote a
tournament in
Dubai.

enough to know that I'm a relaxed guy,' said Federer. No one should expect two men in competition for Grand Slam titles to become close friends, but Djokovic and Federer had been more than civil to each other, even cordial. Indeed, the Serbian even solicited parenting tips before the arrival of his first child. This was not a rivalry with all the poison and animosity of the McEnroe–Connors confrontations. Becker's contention that Federer was 'trying to portray an impossible image' did not go down well. You cannot fake much backstage in tennis, in the locker room, with the players gathered together in the same space. Aside from the match court it is where the players are at their most fried, fraught and frazzled, at their most emotional. These comments, which Federer called 'unnecessary', would have been unwelcome enough from any figure in tennis, but they would have hurt a little more because they came from Becker. 'Of course, I didn't like what he said,' Federer responded. 'After all, he was once my idol.'

There have also been suggestions of tensions between Federer and Murray. Those stories started around the time in 2008 when Murray defeated Federer at a tournament in Dubai. Afterwards, Federer remarked how the Briton's style might lead to him having to 'grind out' victories in the future. If that sounded in any way unflattering, it was not supposed to. Federer's intention had been to offer some constructive criticism about how Murray could give himself the best possible chance of winning the biggest titles. It was said before the Australian Open final against Murray in 2010 that Federer was the most elegant trash-talker in tennis, and perhaps across sport. But surely Federer had just been joking when he said that Murray would be attempting to win Britain's first men's Grand Slam singles title 'for 150,000 years'. Despite what you might hear from some of the armchair psychologists, this was, and is, a civil relationship. How could it be anything else when Murray has spoken of Federer being 'The Greatest'? Besides, according to Federer's former coach Paul Annacone: 'Roger has always had the utmost respect for Andy.' Annacone went on: 'I've read some of the things that have been written, but as Pete Sampras used to say, "Believe nothing of what you read and half of what you see". It makes for much better reading, and some might say a more competitive environment, if there is animosity between the players. But really my feeling is that they get along just fine.'

Such has been the quality of the tennis Federer and Nadal have produced over the years, there has been no need for any Connors–McEnroe-style animosity to sell the rivalry to the public. The pair have been appreciated as tennis players rather than tennis grotesques. One year, when Nadal was playing at a tournament in Basel, and Federer could not compete because of injury, the Swiss turned up at his rival's hotel and knocked on the door to say hello, just because it seemed like the right thing to do. On other occasions Federer has given Nadal a ride in his jet. Why would Federer not get along with a rival who addressed him variously as 'Roger', 'Rogelio' and 'the greatest ever'? And who once said this about Federer's game: 'He's the perfect player. Perfect serve. Perfect volley. Super perfect forehand. Perfect backhand. Very fast on court. Everything is perfect.'

When Federer cried after losing the 2009 Australian Open final, Nadal put a consoling arm around him. Of course, there have been a few bumps along the way, such as when Federer looked over at Nadal's uncle Toni during a final at Rome's Foro Italico and suggested that he was illegally coaching his nephew: 'Everything all right, Toni?' And no doubt Federer, who likes to play quickly, would prefer it if Nadal did not take quite so much time between points. But when you consider what has been at stake when they have played, the pair have been enormously pally towards each other. Rather, it has been small numbers of opposing supporters, the closest modern tennis comes to tribalism, who have been the most vociferous and sulphurous in their exchanges. 'To be a Federer fan was to be an anti-fan of Nadal,' the tennis historian Elizabeth Wilson wrote. 'The Spaniard bounds on to court like a bull, a muscle-bound thug with a hefty bottom, dressed (in the early years) like Freddie Mercury in sleeveless tops that showed off biceps the size of Tim Henman's head. In play, he glowered, he snarled, he glared, he grunted, he scowled.'

Andy Roddick is direct and open and holds no fear of confrontation. That was clear one wild summer in New York when he pushed Djokovic up against a locker. With Federer, though, he could do nothing but like the guy who kept demolishing his tennis. Hence the time he strode up to Federer in the locker room and said: 'I'd love to hate you, but you're too nice.' A few years later, with Roddick retired, he spoke of how there was no side to Federer. Often, Roddick said, you can look at how a public figure is presented and wonder whether the reality lives up to the hype. But he said with Federer he truly was as polite and as pleasant as he was made out to be. There are not two Roger Federers, Public Roger and Private Roger, but just the one. That helped Roddick to deal with the 'torture' that Federer put him through. Roddick's failure was the same

SEASON-ENDING CHAMPIONSHIPS

Six titles in nine years

2003 | 2004 | 2005 | 2006 | 2007 | 2008 | 2009 | 2010 | 2011

In 2017, Federer became the first man to qualify for the tournament 15 times.

Federer has won 81 per cent of the matches he has played at the tournament, more than anyone apart from Ilie Nastase (88 per cent).

81%

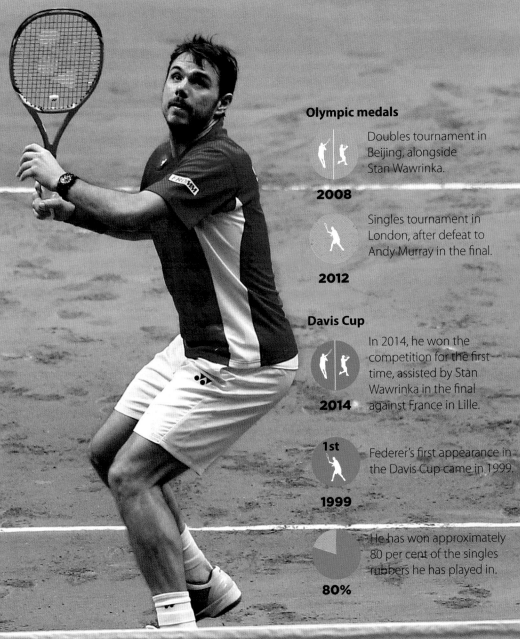

Olympic medals

Doubles tournament in Beijing, alongside Stan Wawrinka.

2008

Singles tournament in London, after defeat to Andy Murray in the final.

2012

Davis Cup

In 2014, he won the competition for the first time, assisted by Stan Wawrinka in the final against France in Lille.

2014

1st

Federer's first appearance in the Davis Cup came in 1999.

1999

He has won approximately 80 per cent of the singles rubbers he has played in.

80%

◄ Federer carries
Switzerland's flag
at the opening
ceremony of the
2008 Beijing
Olympics.

as everyone else's failure: he could not find anything objectionable about Federer that might concentrate the mind.

Much was made of the episode at the 2014 end-of-season tournament in London when Mirka Federer appeared to call out at her husband's semi-final opponent, Stan Wawrinka. Within a few days Federer and Wawrinka were united again as they prepared for the Davis Cup final against France, and posed together for a group photograph in which Wawrinka stood behind Federer making 'bunny ears'. No sign, in that image, of any lingering tensions, and together Federer and Wawrinka had one of the most fulfilling weekends of their careers. The ATP World Tour does not mobilise the vote for the Stefan Edberg Sportsmanship Award: no one is forcing Federer's contemporaries to keep propelling him to victory. That is entirely their choice. 'This is a classy sport, and I try to represent it as well as I can,' said Federer, a former president of the ATP Player Council, as well as the sport's leading ambassador. His peers know that is not him being a fake or a phony. Just days before the Wawrinka episode Federer had been presented with the Sportsmanship Award for a tenth time, a moment made even more special by Edberg making the presentation on court.

Behind the scenes, Federer is also known for his sense of fun. Take the time when, as he walked to a press conference in Cincinnati, having just won the final, he took one of the walkie-talkies used by the tournament staff and broadcast this message across the site: 'The eagle has left the nest'. Pete Sampras saw some of that Federer silliness on that mini-tour of Asia when he would sidle up to people and blow in their ears. On another occasion Federer was singing in the locker-room showers and, according to American journalist Jon Wertheim, 'after being urged to pipe down, he would emerge to do full Pavarotti histrionics'. When no one is watching Federer's training sessions, and that does not happen very often, he loves to be 'a clown' on the practice court. Federer was once involved in a fifteen-minute tennis-ball fight in the locker room at one of the Masters-level events, and, according to one witness, a tournament mascot chose the wrong time to walk in and was caught in the cross-fire.

Sometimes, Mirka has been the victim of Federer's humour. One night at a Japanese restaurant he smeared a dangerous amount of wasabi paste under a piece of sashimi on her plate. Mirka, who had not noticed the sabotage, swallowed the fish and Federer watched and smiled as 'the fire came out of her nose'.

10

THE ROCK, THE PRAM AND THE BILLIONAIRE-IN-WAITING

THE IMAGE OF FEDERER VACUUMING THE CARPETS CAUSED
CONSIDERABLE AMUSEMENT IN CERTAIN QUARTERS. SOME
COULD NOT QUITE DEAL WITH THE IDEA OF THE GREATEST
TENNIS PLAYER IN HISTORY DOING SOMETHING SO MUNDANE.

'A travelling circus' was how Roger Federer once described his life on the road. So one of the first things he does on being shown to that week's hotel suite is to arrange what you might call 'The Children's Corner'. Moving from one hotel to another could potentially be bewildering for the Federers' children – identical twin daughters Myla Rose and Charlene Riva, and non-identical twin boys Leo and Lenny – so they ensure that one part of every room they stay in is always the same. The arrangement of toys helps the children feel they are in a familiar environment. Structured days and regular daily routines also allow them to make sense of the nomadic lifestyle. Even when Federer is not with his children, because of a match, a practice session or some other commitment, he will know what they are doing at all times. When Federer is around he is very much a hands-on father. If his children are ill he will not hold back on the cuddles. 'If I get sick as well,' Federer has said, 'that's too bad.' As Federer puts it, his children have been educated around the world, and have grown up on the Tour. Even while preparing for the US Open one summer, Federer found time to take his family to a Broadway show, *Finding Neverland*, and was so moved by the performance that he 'cried like crazy'. 'What's wrong with you?' the children asked, to which he could only answer, through laughter as well as tears: 'I don't know.'

If Federer had not felt able to travel the circuit with his family, it is a moot point whether he would have continued to take such pleasure from his tennis. Or whether he would have continued to play at all, after the birth of his daughters in the summer of 2009, and his sons, who arrived in the spring of 2014. While Federer and Mirka have the means to travel regularly by private jet and employ nannies, those luxuries do not necessarily mean that family life

▶ Federer
married Mirka at
a small ceremony
in Basel in 2009.

out on the Tour always runs in a straightforward way. 'Yes, Roger travels first-class, if not in his own jet,' Boris Becker said, 'but I'm sure there are challenges with the kids adapting to time changes and also the climate changes.' But somehow the Federers have found a way of making it work. In part because spending time with his family has allowed Federer to make sense of the madness of his celebrity. And this is true whether that is on the road, at home in Switzerland or Dubai, or perhaps on a hike in the Swiss mountains.

No doubt it helps that Federer is a gregarious man who likes having people around him. Federer's family are with him at almost all the tournaments he plays, though there is the occasional week when he travels without his wife, children or any friends. On those occasions he has been known to pass spare hotel room keys to members of his team, along with an invitation: 'Just come by.' 'I love having an open house at the hotel or in my place,' Federer told *Sports Illustrated*.

Domestic duties are part of Federer's routine. In between his Centre Court performances at Wimbledon, for instance, he will help clean the house that he rents for the tournament. 'It's just part of the grind, you know,' Federer said, and the image of him vacuuming the carpets or putting the wheelie bins out for collection caused considerable amusement in certain quarters. Some could not quite deal with the idea of the greatest tennis player in history doing something so mundane. However, these chores do not intrude on Federer's preparations and training, and Mirka ensures that he is sufficiently rested. Sleep is important to every athlete, even to a father of four. When the time comes to get up, Federer does not just want to feel as though he could leap out of bed, he wants to be so refreshed that he feels like 'jumping out of my skin'.

It is Mirka, once described by Federer as 'the rock in my corner', who has enabled him to lead this 'circus' life after the birth of their children, and to make the most of his tennis talent. Even before they became parents, Mirka was a much more influential figure than your average tennis 'other half', helped by the fact that she had also been a professional tennis player. Born in the Slovakian part of Czechoslovakia in 1978, Miroslava 'Mirka' Vavrinec is three years older than Federer. She was a toddler when her family fled communism for a new life in Switzerland. While her parents ran a jewellery shop, a young Mirka had dreams of becoming a ballerina. That was until the family went to watch another émigré from Czechoslovakia, Martina Navratilova, who was competing in a tournament in Filderstadt in Germany. They happened to strike up a conversation with Navratilova, who urged Mirka to try tennis. Actually, she went further than that: this serial Grand Slam champion went to the trouble of arranging Mirka's first tennis lesson. Very quickly it became apparent that Mirka had the talent and physique to excel at the sport, and her ambition was to play professionally. She also did not lack determination or, as she called it, stubbornness. She showed this side of her nature in the 1990s when she travelled by bus to a tournament in Croatia. The journey took her past burnt-out villages and vehicles that had been torched during the Balkan War. It was a terrifying journey, but one she was prepared to make.

It was during the 2000 Sydney Olympics that Federer and Mirka became a couple. Why, Mirka had been wondering, had Federer been so interested in hanging around her? After all, had Federer not said he would choose tennis over having a girlfriend? And then, on the last day of the Games, he kissed her

◀ Mirka has played a huge part in Federer's success.

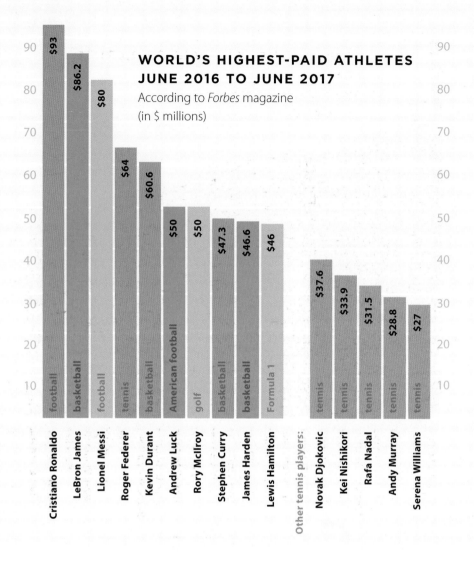

Athlete	Sport	Amount
Cristiano Ronaldo	football	$93
LeBron James	basketball	$86.2
Lionel Messi	football	$80
Roger Federer	tennis	$64
Kevin Durant	basketball	$60.6
Andrew Luck	American football	$50
Rory McIlroy	golf	$50
Stephen Curry	basketball	$47.3
James Harden	basketball	$46.6
Lewis Hamilton	Formula 1	$46
Other tennis players:		
Novak Djokovic	tennis	$37.6
Kei Nishikori	tennis	$33.9
Rafa Nadal	tennis	$31.5
Andy Murray	tennis	$28.8
Serena Williams	tennis	$27

for the first time. At the time of that kiss Mirka had less than two years left of her career, though at least in that time she was able to compete alongside Federer in the Hopman Cup, an international team event in Perth that players use to prepare for the Australian Open. Her last competitive appearance came in the first round of qualifying for a clay-court tournament in Budapest in 2002, for which she was paid $150. At the age of twenty-four, and with life-time prize-money just north of a quarter of a million dollars, Mirka retired, unable to continue because of damaged ligaments in her foot. While her ranking had peaked at seventy-six, and she had made the third round of a Grand Slam with a run at the 2001 US Open blocked by Belgium's Justine

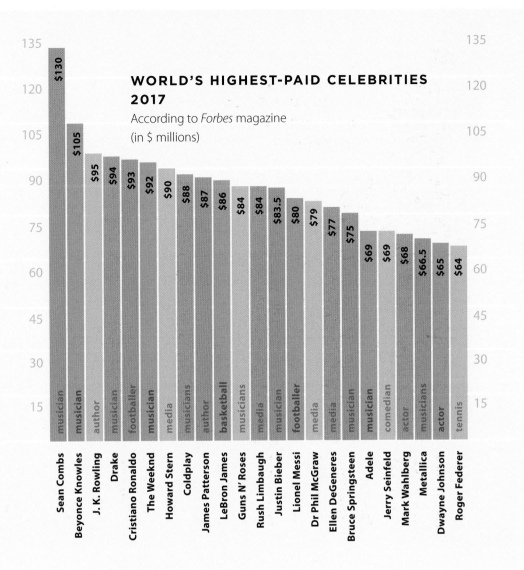

WORLD'S HIGHEST-PAID CELEBRITIES 2017

According to *Forbes* magazine
(in $ millions)

Sean Combs	musician	$130
Beyonce Knowles	musician	$105
J. K. Rowling	author	$95
Drake	musician	$94
Cristiano Ronaldo	footballer	$93
The Weeknd	musician	$92
Howard Stern	media	$90
Coldplay	musicians	$88
James Patterson	author	$87
LeBron James	basketball	$86
Guns N' Roses	musicians	$84
Rush Limbaugh	media	$84
Justin Bieber	musician	$83.5
Lionel Messi	footballer	$80
Dr Phil McGraw	media	$79
Ellen DeGeneres	media	$77
Bruce Springsteen	musician	$75
Adele	musician	$69
Jerry Seinfeld	comedian	$69
Mark Wahlberg	actor	$68
Metallica	musicians	$66.5
Dwayne Johnson	actor	$65
Roger Federer	tennis	$64

Henin, she felt she could have accomplished much more. In her words, she fell into a 'deep hole' of despair. 'It's not easy when you do something you like your entire life and then suddenly one day you have to quit,' she recalled. It was Federer who brought her out of it. As Mirka once told the Swiss journalist René Stauffer: 'Roger was my greatest support back then. He gave me my tennis life back. When he wins, it's as if I win as well.' Mirka's life changed quickly. Little more than a year after she retired, her boyfriend became Wimbledon champion. Within a couple of years he was dominating tennis.

Mirka has discovered she can be a more influential figure from the side of the stadium than she ever was when she was out there competing. Federer

values Mirka's insights on strategy and technique. There were times, before they had children, when she would sometimes step in as a practice partner. That tended to be on the morning of a final, when everyone else but Federer's opponent had left town and he needed someone to warm him up before play. There was a stage when Federer and Mirka had almost every meal together and when she attended practice sessions as well as his matches. 'No other woman,' Mirka once said, 'could deal with so much tennis.' Mirka's role was not restricted to prepping Federer for his matches. For a while he did not have an agent, manager or diary secretary, so Mirka was deputed to organise his life by taking care of his media commitments, as well as travel arrangements and other business. Even when Federer turned to a management company, he still involved her in everything, including choosing his entrance music at the US Open. Her importance did not go unnoticed, and one spring a group of fans arrived at the clay-court tournament in Monaco dressed in playful 'Mirka is the boss' T-shirts.

If a pram in the hallway is the enemy of good art, a buggy in the hotel lobby is supposedly a barrier to realising your tennis ambitions. And it is true there are a number of greats – with Sampras, Ivan Lendl, John McEnroe and Stefan Edberg among them – who did not win a single major as fathers. But domesticity has hardly acted as a restraint on Federer's ability. In fact, it has probably energised him. The day the scan showed Mirka was expecting twins, Federer felt as though he had 'wings' and pulverised Juan Martín del Potro in the quarter-finals of the 2009 Australian Open for the loss of just three games. On Easter Saturday that year the Federers married in a small, private ceremony at a Basel registry office. 'It was a very special moment,' Federer said. 'I had thought it was going to be a lot more relaxed since we had been together for a long time, and that once you are married not a whole lot would change, but it definitely does change your mindset, your life. I got very emotional. It was just nice to know that she loves me so much, and that I love her very much.'

The honeymoon could have been better. Federer took a wild card into the clay-court tournament at the Monte Carlo

◀ Federer at a launch party for the year-end championships in London.

▶ Federer greets his family after winning a tournament.

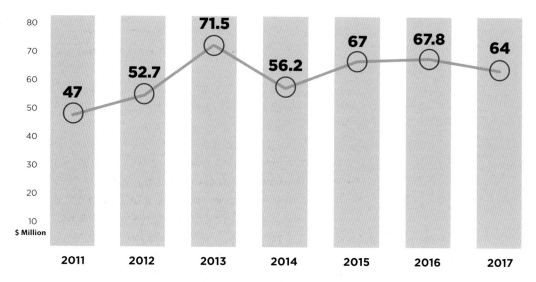

80 —
70 —
60 —
50 —
40 —
30 —
20 —
10 —
$ Million

47 — 2011
52.7 — 2012
71.5 — 2013
56.2 — 2014
67 — 2015
67.8 — 2016
64 — 2017

FEDERER'S INCOME, YEAR BY YEAR
According to *Forbes* magazine.

Country Club and lost early on against Stan Wawrinka. But a few months later he would achieve two of the most important victories of his career by winning the French and Wimbledon titles. Within days of that Wimbledon victory, when a fifteenth slam had made Federer the most successful man in the sport's history, Mirka gave birth to twin daughters. The couple called it 'the best day of our lives'. There were challenges in travelling the globe with two young children, not least because of the pushchair, nappies and extra luggage they now had to take with them. And Federer was concerned that he would have to practise first thing in the morning so he could come back to help Mirka. But Federer should not have been so concerned. There was no need for dawn training sessions – how would he have found practice partners at that hour? – and the other practical challenges were not insurmountable. Six months after becoming a father, Federer won another Grand Slam at the 2010 Australian Open. Indeed, his first major as a dad almost came sooner than that as he led Juan Martín del Potro two sets to one in the final of the 2009 US Open. Federer's second Grand Slam as a father came at the 2012 Wimbledon Championships.

FOR ALL DJOKOVIC'S SUCCESS ON THE COURT, HE HAD NO CHANCE OF CHALLENGING FEDERER'S DOMINANCE OFF IT, ESPECIALLY AT THE LUXURY END OF THE MARKET WHERE FEDERER'S PARTNERS HAVE INCLUDED A CHAMPAGNE HOUSE, A SWISS WATCH-MAKER AND A PRIVATE AIR TRAVEL COMPANY.

Twins run in the family, with Federer's sister Diana also the mother of a set. The birth of Leo and Lenny prompted one British bookmaker to offer odds of ten thousand-to-one against an all-Federer mixed doubles final at Wimbledon at some stage in the future. Their arrival also brought on a surge in form for Federer: he made the final of Wimbledon in 2014 and threatened the world number one ranking. Such was Federer's apparent mastery at being a father and a tennis player that when Novak Djokovic learned his wife was pregnant he asked the Swiss for advice on how to handle it. One of Federer's motivations for continuing to compete was that he wanted his children to be old enough to remember watching him play. That was certainly the case at the 2015 Wimbledon Championships, when the Federer girls were approaching their sixth birthdays. However, not unnaturally they were unsure about the significance of what they were watching, and apparently had not quite worked out the difference between a practice session and a match. What they did know, though, was that they wanted Daddy to win. And to avoid sunburn. Later that summer, in the minutes between winning a tournament in the Cincinnati heat and the start of the prize-giving ceremony, Federer walked over to embrace his family, and his children plonked a baseball cap on his head. 'Papa, you need to wear a hat.'

●

When he gets there, Roger Federer will not be tennis's first billionaire. That honour goes to Ion Țiriac, a former French Open quarter-finalist who went on to shape the careers of Ilie Năstase, Boris Becker and Goran Ivanišević. He has owned his own bank and airline, and in 2015 re-entered a global list of dollar billionaires compiled by *Forbes* magazine. It is thanks to the Romanian, incidentally, that Federer has the distinction of winning a tournament on blue clay: the businessman owns an event in Madrid, and thought that a change in colour would generate more coverage. That it did, but there were so many complaints about the quality of the surface that the ATP World Tour was compelled to have the event switch back to conventional terracotta. Often seen taking up residency in the President's Box on Court Philippe Chatrier during the French Open, Ţiriac is still very much part of the tennis landscape. And yet most of Ţiriac's wealth has been generated by the businesses he established after tennis in post-communist Romania. So, Ţiriac was the first to a billion, but Federer could become the first player to make a billion dollars primarily from swinging a racket.

Federer has won more than $100 million in career prize-money, and yet that is only one part of his income, and a minor part at that. Analysis by *Forbes* showed that Federer was the fifth highest-paid athlete in the world. With an income of $64 million in the twelve-month period from June 2016 to June 2017, Federer trailed only footballer Cristiano Ronaldo ($93 million), basketball's LeBron James ($86.2 million) and footballer Lionel Messi ($80 million). That was not the most lucrative twelve months of Federer's career. That came between June 2012 and June 2013 when he had earned $71.5 million, though that figure was inflated by an off-season exhibition tour of South America for which he is believed to have been paid $14 million for six nights' work across three different cities.

Breaking down Federer's $64 million, $6 million came from prize-money and $58 million from a combination of sponsorship contracts and fees to appear at exhibitions and tournaments. It is true that every tennis player of note will earn more from endorsements than prize-money, but never before to this extent.

Many of Federer's sponsors are at the luxury end of the market, including a Champagne house, a Swiss watchmaker and a private air travel company. On becoming an ambassador for Moët & Chandon, Federer spoke of 'following in the footsteps of Scarlett Johansson, which is quite an honour' and of 'feeling part of a glamourous tradition'. Clearly, Federer does not need to dominate tennis as he once did to maintain his deal flow, with Kurt Badenhausen, a senior editor at *Forbes* magazine, saying: 'Roger has a certain elder statesmen appeal.'

As counter-intuitive as it might sound, it was Federer's decision not to chase money as a young man that would help him to accumulate such wealth in later years. Some teenagers aspire to great riches; Federer did not. That was why his mother, Lynette, was so astonished when she read an interview in a local newspaper in which her son, then a schoolboy without a driving licence, when asked what he would buy with his first prize-money cheque, replied: 'A

Mercedes.' She could not believe he would have given such an answer, and asked the journalist if she could listen to the recording of the conversation. It turned out that what he had actually said in Swiss–German was: *'Mehr CDs'*. More CDs.

As he became more successful, and companies made him offers, Federer said he felt athletes were judged as much on the quality of their sponsors as on their accomplishments. He was adamant that he 'didn't want to sign deals just to have deals'. It was far more important, he thought, that he had more time to train and to play, and to be 'free in the mind'. In those early days he imagined that being a tennis player meant training hard, hearing the roar of the crowd on Centre Court, perhaps doing the occasional interview, and popping in here and there for the odd personal appearance. He had not spent much time considering the business side of the game.

For a while during his prime, Mirka acted as his manager, and he would consult his parents, as well as a lawyer, about any commercial decisions that needed to be made. Federer, whose childhood holidays had included safaris in South Africa, called this close group of advisers, 'The Hippo Company'. His parents were also involved in the important business of answering fans who wanted autographed photographs; for a good number of years, anyone who wrote to Robert and Lynette Federer at their home address on the website would receive a signed picture within a month. 'When Roger's career took off in 2003, he was just ending his contract from International Management Group,' someone close to the Federer camp said. 'From 2004 to the fall of 2005, he didn't have an agency to represent him, though at the end of that period, he chose to work again with I.M.G. During that time without an agency he had an in-house management team, built around his family. In hindsight, this was a blessing. When he had started to dominate the Tour, he almost hadn't signed any contracts, since he and his parents always had the policy to have only a few, but very high quality, partners. And then, when he returned to I.M.G., his market value and reputation was already that high, and they could basically choose their partners and get huge contracts.'

On returning to I.M.G., Federer was taken on by Tony Godsick, an American married to former Grand Slam finalist Mary Joe Fernández, who had risen to prominence through his work with Monica Seles. Such is the bond that has developed between Federer and Godsick's family that Federer has been known to call his agent's son, Nicholas, before he plays to pass on some

'SWITZERLAND IS A SMALL COUNTRY WITH WHICH ONE ASSOCIATES LOYALTY, LUXURY, PRECISION AND PERFECTION. NOW, WHETHER HE'S IN FRANCE, ASIA OR THE UNITED STATES, HE'S WELCOMED AS THOUGH HE IS AT HOME. IT'S AS THOUGH HIS COUNTRY'S NEUTRALITY MAKES HIM A GLOBAL CITIZEN.'

tips. On those occasions Godsick has his own advice for his son: never, ever tell anyone he has received a pre-match pep-talk from Federer, not least because no one would believe him. In 2013, after both their contracts with I.M.G. ran down, Federer and Godsick established their own management company, Team8, with the backing of investors, including Dirk Ziff, an American financier and billionaire. In addition to representing Federer, the boutique company also looks after the interests of other athletes, including tennis players Grigor Dimitrov and Juan Martín del Potro. For as long as Federer continues to play he will essentially be a client of the company. But the opportunity will be there, once he has retired, to take more control in shaping the business. 'Look,' Godsick has said to Federer, 'you're really successful on the tennis court but, I promise you, you will be more successful when you're done playing tennis.'

The cautious approach that characterised his youth has continued. 'Roger will only work with brands that mean something to him,' said a key figure on the Swiss tennis scene. That means only companies who fit in with how he sees himself and his place in the world. For instance, when Moët & Chandon approached Federer, he spent a while mulling it over. With hindsight he wonders what took him so long. Another important consideration is how many days he will need to give to a prospective sponsor, and whether he can spare that time in his already busy schedule. But once Federer has committed to a commercial partnership he does whatever he can to make it work, including providing creative input. Federer cares deeply about ensuring that his partners are benefiting from their collaboration. Note, for instance, how on finishing a final, one of his first acts after shaking hands with his opponent and the umpire is to put a Rolex watch on his wrist.

In addition to the money, Federer also receives exposure in markets where he does not play. The calendar of sanctioned tournaments hardly changes from year to year, with Federer competing in the same cities and markets as he did the season before. While there are opportunities to play exhibitions, such as in India for the International Premier Tennis League where his fees are said to be in excess of a million dollars a night, he cannot be everywhere at one time. That is where his partners can help him to build the brand through marketing and advertising campaigns, though what sells Federer better than anything are live images of him playing tennis on television. Most of Federer's contracts are as long as ten years, which might be viewed as a risk in an era when, in Badenhausen's words, 'athletes are embarrassing their sponsors by appearing in the tabloids and police blotters'. But really, where is the risk with Federer? His life is scandal-free.

'Federer and his team have taken the right approach to maximising his off-court earnings, and I don't think that approach has changed much over the past ten years,' Badenhausen said. 'They have consistently focused on long-term deals with global brands that can take advantage of Federer's global appeal. Federer is the total package for companies as a highly accomplished, attractive, consistent and poised player in a global sport with fantastic demographics for its fanbase. They haven't made any mistakes – I can't think of one.'

Some, and Godsick is among them, would suggest that Federer's nationality has been an important part of his commercial success. 'What makes Roger so attractive to all the big companies is the fact he's Swiss,' Godsick said. 'Switzerland is a small country with which one associates loyalty, luxury, precision and perfection. Now, whether he's in France, Asia or the United States, he's welcomed as though he is at home. It's as though his country's neutrality makes him a global citizen.'

What if the more important factor was not his nationality, but his home city? Growing up in Basel, you cannot help but have an international outlook, especially with the city's airport being over the border in France. As Federer's parents have observed, you can have breakfast in Switzerland, play golf in Germany, sit down to lunch in France, and think very little of it. The borders are essentially irrelevant. And what of Robert and Lynette Federer's choice of name for their son, which they selected, in part, because it is easy to pronounce in English? Badenhausen, though, is not sure that Federer's passport has been key. 'I don't think being Swiss has necessarily helped his international appeal, but I do think that his ability to speak multiple languages fluently opens him up to opportunities that others might not have.'

No sportsman is interviewed as much as Federer. That ability to speak four languages – English, German, Swiss–German and French – means his post-match media commitments at Grand Slam tournaments can last an hour or more for a routine match, and up to three or four hours if he wins the

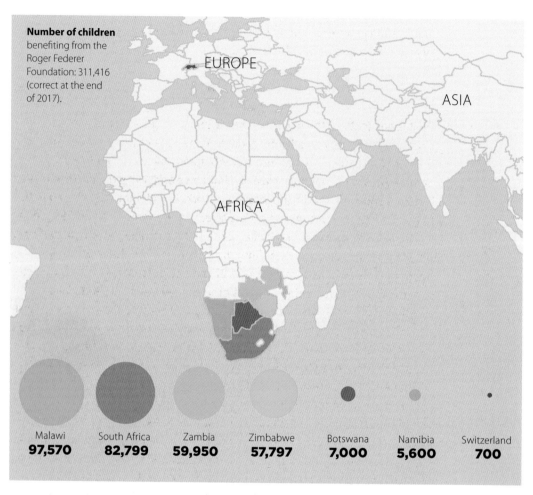

Number of children benefiting from the Roger Federer Foundation: 311,416 (correct at the end of 2017).

EUROPE

ASIA

AFRICA

Malawi	South Africa	Zambia	Zimbabwe	Botswana	Namibia	Switzerland
97,570	**82,799**	**59,950**	**57,797**	**7,000**	**5,600**	**700**

THE ROGER FEDERER FOUNDATION

tournament. In addition to a general news conference in English, and then a separate chat with the Swiss media, Federer also does television and radio interviews. No wonder Godsick teases Federer that it is just as well he does not speak Italian.

But perhaps passports do matter. One key figure in the tennis industry said that if Federer had held a different passport he would now be considerably richer, with his annual endorsement income increased by a multiple of two or even three. 'If Roger had been born American,' he said, 'perhaps he would be a billionaire already.'

●

Established in 2003, the Roger Federer Foundation set itself the target of improving the lives of a million children. At the time of writing it was around a quarter of the way to that number after helping children in South Africa, Zambia, Botswana, Namibia, Malawi, Zimbabwe and Switzerland. When one of Federer's sponsors, Credit Suisse, started working with him, they also agreed to pay his foundation a million dollars a year for ten years. Federer's decision to focus on Africa was informed by his heritage: his mother is South African, his parents met in the country, and they would often return there for family holidays. Federer himself has a South African passport. 'Roger is very involved with the foundation, not just with his time, but also with his heart,' chief executive Janine Händel said. 'It's something that is part of his personality and part of his character. That's why this is so credible – this is not an image thing. As a child, when he went on holidays to South Africa and saw the poverty, he realised that not everybody is raised with the same privileges that he had. It's all about the kids and improving their lives.'

Federer attends every board meeting and no strategic decision is taken without his say-so. The most important time he gives to his foundation, though, is when he visits Africa to see how the money is being spent. On one such trip to Malawi, which came a few days after he lost the 2015 Wimbledon final to Novak Djokovic, he spoke of how it was possible to feel sad and sentimental. But Federer also feels refreshed by these trips, and grateful to have 'spent time with those amazing kids'.

To make the children laugh, Federer held a banana under his nose, pretending it was a moustache that curled up at the ends. Then the banana was turned upside down so it became a sad face. More giggling from the kids. 'Roger just feels so at home and so alive out there and has a good time with the kids,' Händel said. 'The funny thing is that the kids don't know who Roger is. They couldn't imagine that you could possibly earn money by having a racket in your hands and making some moves.'

11

THE YEAR OF THE G.O.A.T.

SIX MONTHS IS A LONG TIME IN THE LIFESPAN OF ANY TENNIS PLAYER, BUT ESPECIALLY FOR SOMEONE IN HIS MID-THIRTIES, WHO HAD NEVER BEFORE HAD SUCH A LONG ABSENCE FROM COMPETITION.

In high-rise Dubai, where hubris and unreality hang in the warm desert air, and where your ambition can easily run away from you, expectations were low. A few weeks before the 2017 Australian Open, his first tournament for six months, Roger Federer was on the practice court when one of his coaches, Severin Lüthi, said to him: 'I tell you, if you play like this, you could win the thing.' If there had been a thought bubble floating above Lüthi's head at that moment, Federer reflected later, it would have read: 'Jeez, you never know.' But Federer did know: he was not going to be the champion in Melbourne. Even for someone of Federer's abilities and past accomplishments, it just was not possible. Federer turned to Lüthi: 'Yeah, I guess so.' If Federer sounded unconvinced, in his head he was even less so. Not for one instant did he take Lüthi's prediction seriously.

Some athletes like to tell you that self-belief makes anything possible, that confidence can overcome any challenge or adversity. That is pretty much Hollywood's take on elite sport: dream big, they say. As it turned out, Federer's run at the Australian Open would be a triumph for thinking and dreaming infinitesimally small. 'This win, it came so far from left field,' Federer has since said. 'I am one hundred per cent truthful when I say that not for one second did I really believe I was going to win.'

Hindsight can give better vision than Hawk-Eye. You can look back at Federer's six-month absence from the courts and say it worked out beautifully, that his break gave him the time to prime his body, technique and spirit before coming back a better player than ever before. Such was Federer's success at Melbourne Park and beyond, it has since appeared as though he started a trend: in 2017, Andy Murray and Novak Djokovic abandoned their

▶ An emotional Federer waves to the Centre Court crowd after winning the 2017 Wimbledon Championships for a record eighth title.

seasons after Wimbledon to heal their bodies, while Stan Wawrinka, Kei Nishikori, Milos Raonic, Tomáš Berdych and Nick Kyrgios also cut short their years, preferring to rest and recuperate rather than playing through injuries. But, going into the Australian Open, there was still a great deal of doubt over the future of a player who had not won a Grand Slam for five years, going all the way back to Wimbledon in 2012. On court in Dubai, amid the desert haze, Federer was peering into the unknown.

Six months is a long time in the lifespan of any tennis player, but especially for someone in his mid-thirties, who had never before had such a long absence from competition. What is more, Federer had not won a tournament in 2016, the first time since 2000 he had ended a year without a title. Who could have known how Federer's game, while functioning well in private sessions, including in practice sets in Dubai against Frenchman Lucas Pouille, would work when he was back facing another member of the 'Big Four' in the Rod Laver Arena?

This was a new experience for Federer and he could not be sure how it would play out. That uncertainty could be traced back to the first operation of his career after he damaged his knee while running a bath for his children during the previous year's Australian Open. Before going under the anaesthetic, he had felt 'nervous and sad about it all'; upon waking from the arthroscopic, or keyhole surgery, he was 'scared'. The pain subsided within a couple of days, and after a couple of weeks Federer had flung aside the crutches. Even so, the doubts seemed to linger, even when he was playing again.

Before the tournament, Federer's view was that Melbourne would come at least three months too soon for him. The expectation was that he would start to reach his peak again around April, while it would not be until Wimbledon in mid-summer that he would be back in contention for the biggest titles again. Winning the Australian Open would be an unimaginable bonus, especially since a month or two earlier Federer had, by his own admission, been 'on one leg' when travelling to Majorca for the opening of Rafa Nadal's academy. With Nadal also suffering from a wrist problem, the pair had only been up to playing a little mini-tennis with the juniors attending the launch. If the opening major of the season went with the seedings, and Federer was seventeenth in the list, the Swiss was not going to venture deep into the fortnight, and would lose in the third round.

It was widely predicted that the title would be won by one of the two younger members of the Big Four: the new number one, Andy Murray, or the defending champion, Novak Djokovic. But, while Federer was fresh for Melbourne, Murray and Djokovic patently were not; both were showing the effects of playing too much tennis towards the end of 2016. Djokovic only lasted as long as the second round, where he was defeated by Denis Istomin, a Uzbek ranked outside the world's top one hundred. That upset was expected to present Murray with a clear run at what would have been his first Australian Open title. But then, in another surprise, Murray also lost early, beaten in the fourth round by Mischa Zverev, a serve-and-volleying German.

The first indication that Federer was playing at a high level had come when he trounced Tomáš Berdych, a former Wimbledon finalist, in straight sets in the third round. Every good story needs a sense of jeopardy, though, and Federer did not have everything his own way on the way to the final: there were five-setters against Japan's Kei Nishikori in the fourth round and fellow countryman Stan Wawrinka in the semi-finals, either side of a more comfortable straight-sets win over Zverev. Then, suddenly, the last men standing were Federer and Nadal.

Every time Federer plays Nadal, the tennis world stops what it is doing and finds either a seat in the stadium or a screen to watch. But when Federer and Nadal met in the final at Melbourne Park it was an encounter of a whole different order. Andy Roddick described it as 'the most important match in Australian Open history, and possibly Grand Slam history'. It was hard to take issue with Roddick. His views were not shouty, empty hyperbole, but thoughtful analysis of what victory would mean for the champion.

The sense was that Federer and Nadal were playing for more than just the trophy. It was to be the first Grand Slam final between the pair since the French Open of 2011, and it felt as though they were competing for historical supremacy, with Federer aspiring to enhance his status as the G.O.A.T. or 'Greatest of All Time'. Walking out on to the Rod Laver Arena that Sunday night, Federer had seventeen majors to Nadal's fourteen. Victory for Nadal would cut Federer's lead to just two, and give the Spaniard some additional momentum before the next Grand Slam, the French Open, where he had been so dominant over the years. Another pertinent fact was that Federer had not beaten Nadal in a Grand Slam final for a decade, going back to their five-setter to decide the Wimbledon Championship in 2007.

◀ Federer in
action at the
Australian Open.

There was tension courtside. Ivan Ljubičić had never been involved in a Grand Slam final before, whether as a player or since becoming Federer's coach at the start of 2016. The Croatian was showing his nerves. Usually, it is the coach who calms a player down before he goes on court, but with Federer and Ljubičić it was the other way round. Ljubičić, along with Lüthi, had done some important work in the weeks building up to the tournament, not least in remodelling Federer's backhand to make it a more aggressive and more potent shot to deploy against all opponents, but particularly against Nadal. For a day and a half before the final, Federer and his coaches discussed in depth and detail the strategy required to defeat Nadal. They had learnt much from watching how Grigor Dimitrov, a Bulgarian with strokes so similar to Federer's he was previously known as 'Baby Fed', prevented Nadal imposing himself on the five-set semi-final. Prepping for the final, Federer knew he had 'weaponised' his backhand. Just as importantly he had a new attacking spirit and verve: he resolved to take the ball early to prevent Nadal controlling rallies with his topspin forehand. As Federer told himself before the final: 'The brave will be rewarded here.' The worst-case scenario was playing too conservatively: keeping the error-count low but losing. 'I didn't want to go down just making shots, seeing forehands rain down on me from Rafa.'

From Nadal's perspective, Federer had 'done something unbelievable' with his backhand. The old Federer might not have found a way out of danger when trailing 1–3 in the final set. Would he have started to fret about how he had not beaten Nadal in a Grand Slam final for ten years? At that moment, it appeared as though Nadal would be the one to get the biggest retro kick from Melbourne Park, with his first Grand Slam title since the 2014 French Open.

During the course of twenty years in elite tennis, Federer has played thousands of games. But it would be difficult to find another handful loaded with as much significance as the ones he won in a row to flip that final set. In the space of a few minutes, as he went from 1–3 to 6–3, Federer gave his best demonstration yet of the combative, competitive spirit that, for years, had tended to be obscured by his genius. Of course, it was still impeccably classy. Not all tennis street-fighting has to follow in the scrappy, gun-slinging style of Jimmy Connors. This was punchy, bold and still wonderfully stylish; tennis that excited the senses. In short, Federer was killing it. An improbable, unexpected Grand Slam triumph was completed in the most spectacular, exhilarating way. Federer's adventure was rewarded with seventy-three winners over the five sets,

FEDERER'S YEAR-END RANKINGS

YEAR	1997	1998	1999	2000	2001	2002	2003	2004	2005	200
RANK	704	301	64	29	13	6	2	1	1	1

▲ Federer's year-end rankings are an illustration of his astonishing longevity – he was just 16 years old when he first finished a season with a world ranking. For 10 seasons in a row, he finished in the top three, including ending five seasons at number one.

more than double Nadal's total. 'I think we were all surprised that Roger won the Australian Open,' his friend Pete Sampras has said. 'To return after such a long break and immediately win a major, that was a pretty incredible feat.'

Every Grand Slam triumph is an emotionally-charged occasion, but this was more special than most. Never one to keep his feelings to himself, Federer cried at the conclusion of a 6–4, 3–6, 6–1, 3–6, 6–3 victory, which had taken three and a half hours. While Federer was generous towards Nadal in his champion's speech, saying: 'We don't have draws in tennis, but if I could have shared this today with Rafa, I would have done', this was an enormously gratifying moment for him. At the age of thirty-five years and 174 days, Federer was the oldest Grand Slam champion since Australian Ken Rosewall, then thirty-seven, won the same tournament in 1972. Other numbers bounced around the Rod Laver Arena: Federer was the lowest-ranked Grand Slam champion since Argentina's Gastón Gaudio, the then world number forty-four, won the French Open in 2004. Reacquainted with the Norman Brookes Challenge Cup for the first time since 2010, Federer had landed his fifth Australian Open and the unprecedented accolade for a male tennis player: winning three different Grand Slam tournaments five times or more.

But no number, however remarkable, could capture the pleasure Federer derived from being a Grand Slam champion again. That night, he 'partied like a rock star'. Back in Switzerland, Federer would take his replica trophy, which he affectionately named 'Norman', up into the mountains; he would also pose with it while lying on some rugs during a photoshoot for GQ magazine, which he later conceded was 'super cheesy'. Whatever happened over the rest of the season, 2017 would be, in Federer's description, 'pure joy'.

●

Knowing your limitations does not sound very sexy, but it was that self-awareness which would help Roger Federer become the most successful man in Wimbledon history. In the early months of 2017, others might have suggested Federer's return was a giddy revival, but he was not getting carried away with himself; complacency has never been an affliction for the Swiss.

Federer's Australian Open win was not a one-off, as he demonstrated in the early spring by taking hard-court Masters titles in Indian Wells and Miami, two of the biggest tournaments after the majors. Significantly, he had not won them both in the same season since 2006. Also noteworthy was that he beat Rafa Nadal at both events: in the fourth round of Indian Wells and then in the Miami final. At that moment, the temptation would have been to keep going through the clay-court season to see if he had it in him to win the French Open for the first time since 2009, and for only the second occasion in all. But Federer was alive to the dangers. Grinding and scuffling on the dirt for a couple of months would only wear out his body and leave him susceptible to injury. Clay-court tennis, after all, is a sport within a sport. The bounce of the ball is different. The tactics are different. The psychologies are different. You have to slide into shots. Playing the Australian Open without a warm-up hard-court tournament was one thing, but it would be quite another to miss all the pre-French Open clay-court tournaments and then drop in for Roland Garros. Besides, the field in Paris would include Nadal, who would go on to win his tenth title there for what was known as 'La Decima'.

So Federer took the decision to skip the clay-court season in its entirety and instead put all his energies into preparing for the All England Club's grass, a surface that suited him far more than Parisian brick-dust. But such a long absence was not entirely without risk. From winning the Miami title in early April to a grass-court event in Stuttgart in mid-June, he did not play at all. And on his opening appearance in Stuttgart, he could not convert a match point and lost to Tommy Haas, a thirty-nine-year-old German ranked 302 in the world. If that had not been part of the plan, he did win his next tournament, at Halle on grass.

Federer's build-up to Wimbledon was very different to the days leading into the Australian Open. Now he was the favourite, which at once seemed both normal and absolutely extraordinary. Here was a father of four, just a month short of turning thirty-six, who would be trying to become the oldest Wimbledon men's singles champion in the Open era. The man Federer was trying to eclipse was Arthur Ashe, who had been thirty-one when he beat Jimmy Connors in the all-American final of 1975. Ashe's victory had been unexpected, born of a game-plan devised on the back of a napkin the night before to take the pace off the ball and give Connors nothing to play with. But everyone knew Federer's tennis would be at the other end of the spectrum. Federer would be playing with verve, ambition, creativity and flair; he would be going for his shots.

Despite the raised expectations, Federer was still able to surprise everyone, including himself, by playing the 'perfect' Grand Slam: going the entire fortnight without dropping a set. Only once before, at the 2007 Australian Open, had Federer achieved that feat, and it had not been done at Wimbledon since Björn Borg in 1976. And this all happened while playing within himself. Federer's Wimbledon performances did not quite touch the heights of his tennis at the Australian Open, and that was simply because he did not need to be at the very limits of his talents to win his second Grand Slam title of the season. Very much the lord of the lawns, Federer was always in control of his own destiny. There was a sense he had at least another level, maybe as many as three, that he could have gone to if necessary. If Federer felt, having missed the French Open, that he was only working 'part-time', he was still vastly superior to all the 'full-time' players who assembled in south-west London.

Given that Federer was playing the best tennis of his career in 2017, it is doubtful the under-performing Andy Murray or Novak Djokovic would have troubled him even if they were at peak form. Just as they were in Melbourne, Murray and Djokovic were reduced figures in London, where they were more obviously constrained by injury. Murray, whose sore hip had put his involvement at risk, hobbled to a quarter-final defeat, while Djokovic retired at the same stage of the tournament with an elbow problem. Apart from a summer cold, Federer was in fine physical shape, and in his eleventh Wimbledon final he met Marin Čilić, a Croatian playing his first.

Born on the eighth day of the eighth month, Federer has confirmed that eight is his favourite number. The morning of the final, he warmed-up with a light session on Court 8. Tears are expected at a Wimbledon final, but it is unusual for a player to sob mid-match, as Čilić did in frustration at the blister on his left foot which meant he was not even close to his best. The match was so one-sided that Federer gave up just eight games for a 6–3, 6–1, 6–4 victory, completed with his eighth ace of the day. His reward was an eighth Wimbledon title, separating him from Sampras and William Renshaw, a giant of nineteenth-century lawn tennis, who won seven each. 'Honestly, I'm incredibly surprised how well this year is going and how well I'm feeling,' Federer disclosed afterwards. 'I knew I could do well again maybe one day, but not at this level. I guess you would have laughed, too, if I told you I was going to win two Grand Slams in a year. People wouldn't have believed me if I had said that. I also didn't believe I was going to win two Slams this year, it's incredible.'

The ease with which Federer won Wimbledon did not diminish the scale of his achievement. On sitting down on his courtside chair, and looking up at his family, including all four of his children, he started to cry. 'They were probably thinking it was a nice view and a nice playground,' said Federer. While not renowned as a hedonist, he recognised that winning a nineteenth Grand Slam, four more than Nadal at the time, was not something to be celebrated with a quiet cup of tea and a slice of lemon drizzle cake. After attending the Champions' Dinner, Federer continued partying with 'thirty or forty friends' in a bar until five in the morning. It was a fuzzy-headed Swiss who, just hours later, returned to the All England Club for a morning round of media interviews, where he would suggest the younger generation should play more aggressively. But any regrets he had over mixing his drinks ('my head's ringing') were quickly soothed by the great thrill of being Wimbledon champion again. Just as he had done with 'Norman' after winning the Australian Open, Federer took his replica Wimbledon trophy up into the mountains of his homeland.

●

Such is the desire in New York City to see Roger Federer and Rafa Nadal play against each other on the US Open's Arthur Ashe Stadium, the boxing promoter Don King once spoke of 'The Grapple in the Apple', a silly marketing slogan that still makes Federer giggle. While Federer and Nadal have met at the other three Grand Slam cities – some of their most enthralling matches

PERFORMANCE

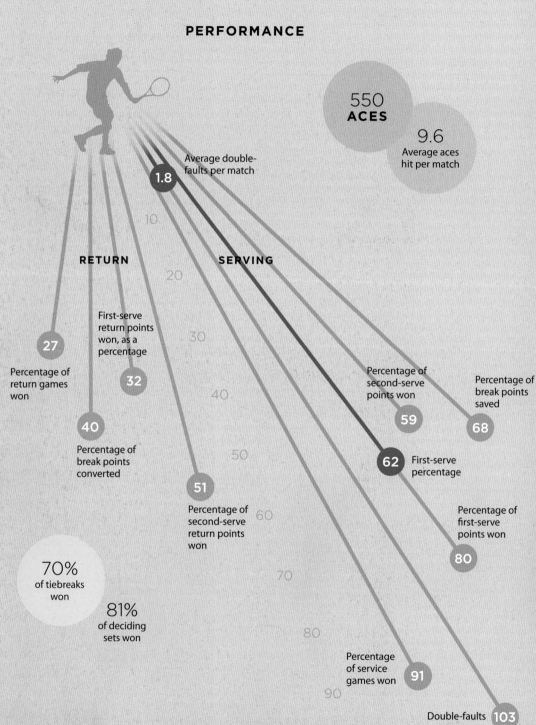

550
ACES

9.6
Average aces
hit per match

Average double-
faults per match
1.8

RETURN   **SERVING**

10

20

First-serve
return points
won, as a
percentage

30

27

Percentage of
return games
won

32

Percentage of
second-serve
points won

Percentage of
break points
saved

59

68

40

Percentage of
break points
converted

40

50

62 First-serve
percentage

51

Percentage of
second-serve
return points
won

60

Percentage of
first-serve
points won

80

70

70%
of tiebreaks
won

81%
of deciding
sets won

80

Percentage
of service
games won

91

90

Double-faults 103

100

2017 BY THE NUMBERS

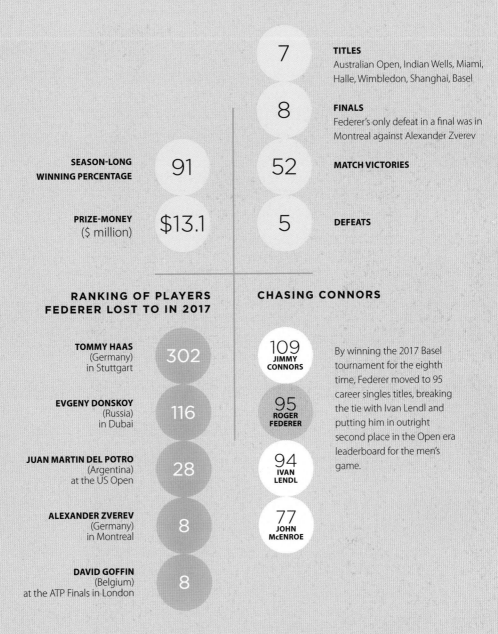

7 TITLES
Australian Open, Indian Wells, Miami, Halle, Wimbledon, Shanghai, Basel

8 FINALS
Federer's only defeat in a final was in Montreal against Alexander Zverev

SEASON-LONG WINNING PERCENTAGE **91**

52 MATCH VICTORIES

PRIZE-MONEY ($ million) **$13.1**

5 DEFEATS

RANKING OF PLAYERS FEDERER LOST TO IN 2017

TOMMY HAAS (Germany) in Stuttgart — **302**

EVGENY DONSKOY (Russia) in Dubai — **116**

JUAN MARTIN DEL POTRO (Argentina) at the US Open — **28**

ALEXANDER ZVEREV (Germany) in Montreal — **8**

DAVID GOFFIN (Belgium) at the ATP Finals in London — **8**

CHASING CONNORS

109 JIMMY CONNORS

95 ROGER FEDERER

94 IVAN LENDL

77 JOHN McENROE

By winning the 2017 Basel tournament for the eighth time, Federer moved to 95 career singles titles, breaking the tie with Ivan Lendl and putting him in outright second place in the Open era leaderboard for the men's game.

have been in finals in Melbourne, Paris and London – they have spent years missing each other at the American slam. New Yorkers are accustomed to getting what they want, and such was Federer's form, and Nadal's own revival, that expectations built all summer that 2017 was the year that this match was finally going to happen.

The first disappointment was how the draw fell: they were both placed in the same half, so any meeting would be in the semi-final and not the title-match. The second, and by far the greatest, was that Federer and Nadal did not grapple at all.

During the summer, between Wimbledon and the US Open, the New York Times produced a profile that neatly summed up 'Federer's twenty-year career tracing the unlikely path of an inverted parabola from unbeatable to unbeatable, with a seven-year stretch of eminently beatable in between'. It was noted that Federer had not lost a match at the Grand Slams for more than a year, going back to his semi-final defeat by Milos Raonic at Wimbledon in 2016. But going into the final major of the year, there was a problem. Federer had felt his back when losing the Montreal final to Germany's Alexander Zverev in mid-August. It led to him withdrawing from the Cincinnati Masters, where he had planned to complete his preparations for Flushing Meadows. The injury made an impact on his performance in the opening round when he needed five sets to defeat Frances Tiafoe, an American teenager then ranked seventy in the world. Federer's next match, against Mikhail Youzhny, was hardly any smoother or more straightforward as he trailed the Russian world number 110 by two sets to one before coming through to win.

One of the more memorable moments of Federer's 2017 US Open did not come in the borough of Queens, but back in Manhattan near his hotel. On a non-match day he chose to practise on the public courts in Central Park, though he probably did not have half as much fun as the New Yorkers having an afternoon hit nearby. Back in Queens, while Federer did not give up a set in the third round against Spain's Feliciano López, or against Germany's Philipp Kohlschreiber in the fourth, he was not in the right physical shape to deal with the power of Juan Martín del Potro in the quarter-finals. The Argentine beat him in four sets, and Federer's considered opinion was that if he had gone through he would not have given eventual champion Nadal much of a match.

Soon after, the pair were back on court together. To honour one of his idols, Federer had created the Laver Cup, a team competition pitching Björn

ALL YEAR, FEDERER
KEPT ON ROUGHING UP
BOTH HIS RIVALS AND
THE PRECONCEIVED
IDEAS OF WHAT A TENNIS
PLAYER IN HIS MID-THIRTIES
IS SUPPOSED TO BE
CAPABLE OF.

Borg's Europe against John McEnroe's 'The World', with the inaugural event staged in Prague. Federer and Nadal played doubles together for the first time, beating the American pair Jack Sock and Sam Querrey. That same weekend, there was even the sight, as Federer sat on his chair during a changeover in a singles match, of Nadal coaching his rival. Almost inevitably, Federer was centre stage at the decisive moment: he saved a match point against Nick Kyrgios, of Australia and 'The World', to give Europe the trophy. From Prague it was on to the final of the following month's Shanghai Masters, where Federer and Nadal reverted to their usual roles: that of opponents. Federer's victory in China meant that, for the first time, he had won five successive matches against Nadal, dating back to a meeting in Basel in 2015.

Landing two Grand Slam titles in 2017 had done much to bolster Federer's status as the greatest player to have ever swung a racket. But the season's head-to-head against Nadal also helped to turn the argument in Federer's favour. It is true they did not play on Nadal's favourite surface, as Federer missed the clay-court season, but Federer's hard-court performances against the Spaniard were exemplary. After their five-setter in the Australian Open, Federer did not drop another set to Nadal all season. Their fourth-round match in Indian Wells was the most one-sided of all, with Federer losing just five games. 'Tactically, he has broken the code,' Mats Wilander, a former world number one, said of the way Federer was approaching his matches with Nadal. Now happy to 'consistently just keep on attacking with the backhand', Federer also suggested that any Nadal-related neurosis had disappeared. 'I just think I'm not so [mentally] scarred like maybe I have been in the past.'

All year, Federer kept on roughing up both his rivals and the preconceived ideas of what a tennis player in his mid-thirties is supposed to be capable of. Federer's seventh title of 2017 came in his birthplace, Basel. After winning the tournament for the eighth time, the former ball-kid at the St. Jakobshalle celebrated in what had become his traditional manner: by treating the current ball-boys and ball-girls to pizza. That success also took him to ninety-five career singles titles, putting him in outright second place in the all-time leaderboard, and trailing only Jimmy Connors on 109.

By opting out of the clay-court season, Federer had missed out on an entire chunk of the calendar, and thousands of ranking points that go with it. Even so, in the final weeks of 2017 it was still mathematically possible for Federer to regain the number one ranking for the first time since 2012, as well as end a season at the top of the standings for the first time since 2009. Considering he had been ranked seventeenth at the start of the year, along with his light schedule, that was astonishing. Never before had a man in his thirties finished a season at the top of the standings. But then, citing the need to rest, Federer withdrew from the Paris Masters, the last tournament before the season finale in London, and the chance had gone. Instead, Nadal, five years Federer's junior at thirty-one, would become the oldest year-end number one in history.

Four months after tearing through the Wimbledon draw, Federer returned to London for the ATP Finals, for which he was the favourite. It is the most exclusive tournament on the calendar, with entry restricted to the most successful eight men of the regular season. Federer had played fourteen years in a row, from 2002 to 2015, before missing the 2016 edition. After qualifying for a record fifteenth time, he was back where he belonged: among the true elite, and attempting to win what would have been an unprecedented seventh title. He already had the tournament record after winning for the sixth time in 2011. Even before play began, Federer picked up three prizes when, at the launch party at the Tower of London, he received two awards voted for by his peers – best comeback and sportsmanship – and one voted for by tennis followers as the most popular player on tour. Astonishingly, that was the fifteenth consecutive year he had won what is known as the 'fans' favourite award'.

Before Greenwich, Federer had lost just four times all season. His first two defeats of 2017 had 'haunted' him for a while, not least because he had three match points against the Russian Evgeny Donskoy in Dubai and one match point against Germany's Tommy Haas in Stuttgart. His back had been causing him discomfort when he lost to another German, Alexander Zverev, in Montreal, and he was not at his physical best at the US Open when beaten by Juan Martín del Potro. Federer went undefeated in his three round-robin matches at the ATP Finals, and progressed to the semi-finals of that tournament for a fourteenth time. His winning percentage for the season at that point was almost at ninety-three.

Federer took the first set in the semi-final against David Goffin before

AT THE END OF A LONG TENNIS YEAR, SOME CAN SOUND EXHAUSTED BY IT ALL, BUT NOT FEDERER. FEDERER'S LOVE FOR THE SPORT, THE SHEER PLEASURE HE TAKES FROM BEING ON COURT, WAS UNDIMINISHED.

losing to the Belgian for the first time in seven meetings. It was the greatest moment of Goffin's tennis life, and Federer's fifth loss of the year, against fifty-two wins. Only once before, when he finished 2005 with a win-loss record of 81–4, had Federer lost fewer matches in a season. The following year, 2006, he also had just five defeats when his tally was 92–5.

Even so, it had been 'an amazing year', and there were no real regrets. Perhaps if Federer had played a few additional tournaments, he would have given himself a strong chance of ending the year as the world number one. But a heavier schedule would also have increased the chance of injury. One of the most pleasing aspects of the year for Federer was how his body had held up. 'Considering how well 2016 went, this year was perfect,' he said. What Federer did not want to do was injure himself and damage his future prospects. Federer closed with a defeat, but he was healthy and happy.

At the end of a long tennis year, some can sound exhausted by it all, but not Federer. Federer's love for the sport, the sheer pleasure he takes from being on court, was undiminished. As his former coach Paul Annacone put it, Federer has 'an indefatigable joy for tennis, but also for life in general'. For Federer, tennis has always been more fun when playing for the biggest titles and on the biggest courts. The tennis equivalent of Off-Broadway – Court 18 at Wimbledon, say – has never held any appeal to him. He would not hit the ball as well on Court 18 as he would on Centre Court. Federer is at his happiest when he is centre stage.

Within minutes of walking off court under the 'tent' in south-east London, Federer was already thinking about 2018. What might he accomplish when it all started up again in January? What did he need to do during the off-season to prepare himself for chasing more Grand Slams? An enduring love for competition and glory, and a lust for elite tennis: ultimately, that lay behind the extraordinary, life-affirming resurgence of Roger Federer.

EPILOGUE

In every tennis player's head, there's a mental game of back-and-forth before the big occasion – these are the rallies that the public never get to see. All day, as he prepared to play in the 2018 Australian Open final that evening, Roger Federer kept on asking himself two questions, and each time he did so it took the pre-match tension to a new, unsettling high.

While supposedly the most relaxed of the four Grand Slams, the scheduling at the Australian Open seems almost designed to make the players fret. Unlike the other major finals, all scheduled in the afternoon, the title-match in Melbourne begins after 7.30pm. Federer, with ambitions of continuing a resurgence that can be traced back to the same tournament in 2017, really did have all day to ask himself: 'How will I feel if I win?' And also, 'How will I feel if I lose?'

While all players have similar conversations with themselves before going out to play in a Grand Slam final, this was different. That night, Federer would have the opportunity to score a twentieth Grand Slam title – one nice round number to go with another, after twenty years as a professional tennis player. With so much on the line, the result would lead to his tearful response after the final – it's not unusual for the Swiss to cry after championship point, or when receiving the trophy, but this was probably the most emotional moment of his tennis life.

Victory over Marin Cilic gave Federer ten per cent of the two hundred Grand Slams played in the Open era. At the age of thirty-six years and 173 days, Federer was the oldest man to take a Grand Slam since Ken Rosewall, then thirty-seven, triumphed at the 1972 Australian Open. On a very hot night, Tennis Australia closed the stadium roof and turned on the air-conditioning. With cries of 'Chum jetze', Federer won 6-2, 6-7, 6-3, 3-6, 6-1 and became the first man, and only the fourth player – after Margaret Court, Serena Williams and Steffi Graf – to win twenty majors or more. 'The fairytale continues', Federer said after achieving parity with Novak Djokovic's six Australian Open men's singles titles, a record for the Open era, and winning his third Grand Slam in twelve months.

Federer's genius was unquestionable that night, and something else was also beyond doubt: how, after two decades of professional play, he didn't just care, but cared more than ever.

BIBLIOGRAPHY

NEWSPAPERS, WEBSITES AND MAGAZINES
ESPN; *Forbes*; *Guardian*; *Independent*; *L'Équipe*; *Mail*; *New York Times*; *New Yorker*; *Observer*; *Sports Illustrated*; *Tages-Anzeiger*; *Telegraph*; *The Times*; *Wall Street Journal*

BOOKS
Agassi, Andre – *Open: An Autobiography*, HarperCollins, 2009
Becker, Boris – *Boris Becker's Wimbledon*, Blink, 2015
Bowers, Chris – *Federer: The Biography*, John Blake Publishing, 2013
Murray, Andy – *Andy Murray: Seventy-Seven: My Road to Wimbledon Glory*, Headline, 2013
Nadal, Rafael & Carlin, John – *Rafa: My Story*, Hyperion Books, 2011
Skidelsky, William – *Federer and Me: A Story of Obsession*, Yellow Jersey, 2015
Stauffer, René – *The Roger Federer Story: Quest for Perfection*, New Chapter Press, U.S., 2004
Wertheim, L. Jon – *Strokes of Genius: Federer v Nadal, Rivals in Greatness*, J.R. Books, 2009

ACKNOWLEDGEMENTS

Above all, I am grateful to Roger Federer for the time he has given me over the years, whether in Melbourne, Miami, Paris or on the telephone. Those conversations have informed *Fedegraphica*, and I have quoted extensively from those interviews. I have also had the opportunity to speak to many of those around Federer, including his parents Lynette and Robert, as well as his coaches Stefan Edberg, Paul Annacone, Madeleine Bärlocher, Seppli Kacovsky and José Higueras, his fitness trainer Pierre Paganini, his stringer-in-chief Nate Ferguson, and some of his friends, including Pete Sampras, Tim Henman and Darren Cahill. Again, those conversations have been invaluable in shaping my thoughts and writings about Federer's tennis life, as was a long-distance call to Australia to speak with Bob Carter, father of the late Peter Carter.

One afternoon in Rome, Novak Djokovic gave me an insight into how he views his encounters with Federer and his relationship with the Swiss. In London I chatted to Boris Becker, once Federer's boyhood idol and lately Djokovic's coach. Some of Federer's other rivals – including Rafa Nadal, Andy Murray, Andy Roddick, Milos Raonic, Richard Gasquet and Thanasi Kokkinakis – have also given me a greater understanding, some of them recently, and others when Federer was in his prime. They enabled me to understand what it feels like to face Federer on the court and to share space with him backstage. I do not believe that Craig O'Shannessy, a coach and analyst, has ever been on court with Federer, but his analysis of Federer's game from courtside is peerless. I am also thankful, in no particular order, to: Rod Laver, Chris Evert, Toni Nadal, Mats Wilander, John McEnroe, Bjorn Borg, Nick Bollettieri, Goran Ivanišević, Kurt Badenhausen, John Yandell, David Bailey, James Buddell, Leo Schlink, Vincent Cognet, Linda Pearce, Theresa Fischbacher, Reto Schmidli, René Stauffer, Colleen Taylor (surely Federer's most devoted fan), Damien Saunder, Nicola Arzani, Simon Higson, Leo Spall, Matt Wilansky, Johnny Perkins, Alexandra Willis, Michael Chang, Siobhan Nicholson, Jamie Renton, Greg Sharko and Martina Hingis.

Many thanks to I.B.M. and the All England Club for their permission to make use of the data from Federer's Grand Slam matches over the years. I have also been reliant on the statistics generated by his performances on the ATP World Tour. Without the creativity and vision of designer Nick Clark, who turned my analysis of that data into the beautiful infographics in these pages, this would be a very different book. I am also indebted to my editor at Aurum, Lucy Warburton, not least because it was her idea to publish a visual biography of Federer. She has provided plenty of direction and encouragement throughout the project. Thanks also to the rest of the team at Aurum, to copy-editor Martin Smith, and to my agents David Luxton and Rebecca Winfield of David Luxton Associates.